NOTES FROM THE LAST BREATH FARM

NOTES FROM THE LAST BREATH FARM

A Music Junkie's Quest to Be Heard

Rob Azevedo

PLAIDSWEDE PUBLISHING
Concord, New Hampshire

Designed and composed at Hobblebush Design, Concord, New Hampshire (www.hobblebush.com)

Printed in the United States of America

ISBN: 978-1-7323648-3-7
Library of Congress Control Number: 2019939033

Front cover by Brendan McCormick

Published by:

PLAIDSWEDE PUBLISHING
P.O. Box 269 · Concord, New Hampshire 03302-0269
www.plaidswede.com

For Mom

CONTENTS

1. NOBODY

"Who do you think you are?"

"Nobody, Mom. Nobody."

"You're damn right you're nobody. And don't you ever forget it."

2. STOP, IN THE NAME OF LOVE

Now, how could I forget those words? *You're damn right you're nobody.* That there is a pretty solid testament. And a stinger to boot. When my mother randomly dropped those bombs on me throughout my youth, they hit me with an iron fist. Arriving with fangs on them, usually in the early morning before I had a chance to clean the crust from my sleepy eyes, those words, they owned me until, well, until they didn't.

Or so I pretend.

Often times, my bedroom door would be kicked open early on a Saturday morning. The window blinds ripped open as the morning sun came rising up, my fiery-tongued Irish born mother, weighing no more than 100 pounds, was fucking Josey Wales in a housecoat, a full-on-fury machine when she chose to be.

Raging and always ready to lay the hammer down, you could sense the mood of the house from the moment you woke from another wretched night sleep, french-kissing with the Sandman.

First, a little eye would appear from under the bedspread. Barely visible, even in the early morning light. The young eye would read the shadows beneath the bedroom door, gathering speed. Soon a small ear would follow from under the covers, listening for my mother's lashing bark.

On those unpredictable dawns when the mood of the day hung in the balance, there was always one thing I could count on: If the house was quiet, well, we were all screwed. That only meant my mother was marinating somewhere about something—a light left on the basement, an unzipped bag of cold cuts wasting away in the crisper, sneaker marks on the hallways rugs lined tighter than the outfield grass at Fenway Park.

You know, the big stuff.

Sometimes during those early hours, my mother would launch into a fit of rage, never quite knowing what she was raging about. But rage she would with the thunderous clap of a thousand lightning storms. It was an impressive show of force for such a slight frame. Frightening and impressive.

But on those precious mornings when the house was filled with the sounds of Motown coming from a small kitchen radio; oh, baby, life was grand. Frankie Valli, The Supremes, Diana Ross, Marvin Gaye, The Ronettes, all those rich voices mixing with the smell of eggs and bacon always provided a beautiful soundtrack to start the day. Those Motown artists had the ability to smooth out the lines in my mother's face and turn a three-minute song into something you couldn't exactly trust, but was sure glad to hear.

For however long it lasted.

I don't remember my mother dancing much around the kitchen to "Stop In The Name Of Love," but I do remember she could carry a tune. And she was proud of her voice. She'd save the chorus of the song to showcase her vocal range, kicking into, *Baby love, my baby love, I need you, oh, how I need you,* as she slid a hot plate of grease in front of my pudgy fingers.

There's just something about Motown music that brings out the crooner in all of us. Even those buried beneath a furnace of life's rank frustrations. As I remember it, my introduction to Motown, that flavor-packed, soulful groove so sweet to the ear, arrived sometime around 1977, when I first heard Arthur Cooney's classic "Sweet Soul Music." And that song, for whatever reason, framed some of my favorite memories of my mother. The ones when she was singing in the kitchen wearing a pleated housecoat, cooking up a morning feast, smoothing out the lines in her face.

3. NO FREE RIDES

She was a great mother, though, and I loved her dearly. Don't let me sell it any other way. I can be a tad difficult myself. She was super organized, spit-shined clean, a barnstorming shopper, an impeccable dresser, a receptionist for a doctor in town and someone who could talk on the phone through a half rack of smokes and never get bored of discussing the bargain sales going on at Filene's Basement that week. Any week for that matter. My mother also made the tastiest damn ham and cheese sandwiches this side of the earth. Something about the way she spread the mayo on the bread was pure art. The perfect coating of cool cream beneath a thin bed of lettuce. Or was it the cheese? Almost crispy is how I remember it tasting. The ham seemed to crunch with moisture.

And even with my mother's hard edges and sometimes caustic manner, she bred me, she fed me, she loved me. Never did I go unbathed, unclothed, unprovided for. Materially, I lived the Life of Riley. My mother booked all the trips to Florida, the short vacations to the Cape, to New Hampshire. She would lend me her 1984 Honda Prelude from time to time, which I blew the transmission out on "Grudge Night" down at the New England Dragway in Epping, New Hampshire, fucking off with my good buddy, Sweet Lou, trying, once again, to be somebody. Not just a big fat "nobody."

My mother also handled the bills, bought the Christmas presents, navigated the parties, shopped for the meats, the fish, the eggs. She would occasionally and ceremoniously press a $20 bill into the palm of my hand (Tony Soprano style) if I was too broke to afford a movie ticket, or a prom corsage, or a birthday gift for my sisters or father or some friend that didn't really like me. She'd press my fist with cash, piercing my knuckles with her rings-covered fingers, searching for bone, I always figured. She would then, and always, let me know that this agreement was, under no uncertain terms, a handout.

4

"No free rides for you, shit bag. I'm running a tab."

And my mother most certainly did start a tab with me. If I remember correctly, while I was at Plymouth State College in the early 1990s, studying English and running up my own tabs at a downtown tavern called the Outback, where I would regularly slap all the cheap beer I could muscle down my gullet onto a Discover Card that was sent to me in the mail. I had no clue how this ridiculous habit of charging all my bad habits (drinking beer, chewing tobacco, eating fast food) was going to vastly alter my near future. I usually just left the credit card at the tavern, for weeks or months even, either forgetting to grab the tab or not caring to sign the receipts. What difference did it make if the bill was $23 or $230 bucks? I didn't have the money to pay it anyways. Never would either. Not for another decade, at least.

But the tickle of doom was always there in the back of my ear, cranking away at my senses during my more sober moments, reminding me in the dark that I couldn't possibly not know that soon this ride would end, and end badly.

And it did.

4. SWAGGERLESS

Months after graduation, I was busted. The credit ran out. I was $6,000 in beer-soaked debt. My mind was broken. And I mean shattered in a million pieces. My confidence was at an all-time low. Whatever swagger I carried myself with during my college years as a Panther had turned to dust. Vanished. I was without an identity, a faceless face in the crowd once again. Nothingness descended upon me like an out of control freightliner. When I drank, I drank too much. Blackouts and all. Didn't eat a vegetable for six months. I had to masterbate in order to fall sleep. I was a driving limos, working as a doorman, a credit collector, a freelance writer. I even delivered animal blood for a living. The list goes on and on.

I had also broken up with the best woman I ever knew (my wife of today, Flower) for no reason whatsoever, after years of being together already. Just for the fuck of it. Still can't explain that move to this very day. Wasn't the booze, not drugs. It was ego, probably. Shithead.

A fragmented mess of a man.
A dreamer doing shit.
Questless.
A straight-up nobody.
Lost at 25.

My mother was indeed a soothsayer, the knower of all things, the three-eyed raven from the east side of town. She predicted I would be a nobody, and holy hell! She was right! I was doing a pretty damn good job at living up to her premonitions. Caked in concrete, my life's quandaries were barely worth romanticizing over anymore.

Barely.

5. COME TO THE DOOR, MA

So, what did I do? I called my mother. Of course I did! I never needed her, I told myself, until I did, right.

That call always reminded me of a song by Bruce Springsteen named "The Hitter."

"Come to the door, Ma, and unlock the chain.
I was just passin' through and got caught in the rain.
There's nothin' I want, Nothin' that you need say.
Just let me lie down for awhile and I'll be on my way."

I remember conceding to this sad state of affairs in a lifeless condo in Manchester, where I lived with my college roommate, Case, who, much like myself, was floundering in a sea of debt. It was late afternoon after another day running from grocery store to grocery store, rotating cases of beer in and out of huge coolers, working as a merchandiser for a beer distributor in Concord. The job was considered gold if you were a newly crowned college graduate and didn't mind talking and hustling. You end up mingling with the the people as a merchandiser, working your arms and legs ripping apart pallets of booze, shouldering the moods of the store managers, and sitting in on sales meetings that actually felt more like a high school football locker room at half-time after a shitty two quarters of play.

Ironically, one of the big bosses, the man who ran some of these meeting at the beer distributor was named Joe Dudek, and Mr. Dudek was a human machine as a running back at Plymouth State College in the mid 1980s, scoring 79 touchdowns during those years. He scored so many touchdowns, once five in one game, for the small Division III football team, that he ended up on the cover of the Sports Illustrated in 1985. He shared the cover titled "What the Heck. Why not Dudek?" with none other than the legendary, Bo Jackson, and a quarterback named Chuck

7

Long, two powerhouse college players that were also being considered for the Heisman Trophy.

Joe lost to Bo, of course, but what a ride, what a story!

Anyhow, I basically drove from one supermarket to the next, all around southern New Hampshire stocking coolers. The added bonus of the job was being able to dust past all the young mothers with their high hip bones who were filling up the hours shopping for chicken, formula, fruits and baby powder. But, that job wasn't for me. I raised the white flag on the gig. Threw it away after six months. Quitting to a surprised manger, who, while looking at me, basically said, "Dipshit, are you stupid? You shouldn't be quittin' anything."

And in many ways, he was right. That 6K debt wasn't going away. I hadn't even made a dent in it. If anything I was slamming more charges onto whatever sucker deal came my way in the mail with a $1,500 line of credit. The collection calls coming into the condo were relentless. The unopened envelopes from creditors across the country were spewing out the kitchen trash can, which was basically a black plastic garbage bag tossed somewhere on the sticky linoleum kitchen floor.

So, like it said, I called my mother and asked her if I could move home. She said, yes. And I didn't even need to beg, not once. "Come home," she said without hesitation. "You can stay in the basement." Sweet! But then, I thought: "What gives? What's with all this emotional generosity?"

This response was out of the norm, a total departure from the woman I knew, the woman who one minute might be running her fingers through my hair, telling me how wonderful a head of lettuce I had while watching "Dallas" together on a Friday night. Then, switch on a dime and accuse me of being the most selfish, lazy eggitt she ever had the displeasure of knowing. Perplexed, I was still thankful that she decided she "showed me a kindness" and let me move back to The Rose.

Had time managed to soften my mother's sharped edges? This is what I wondered.

Not always, but often, it was always a dance with my mother, a never-ending head game. More than I could handle as a kid, and, I suppose, more than I could handle as a young adult. At times, yes, she seemed to take pleasure in reminding me where I stood in this world. *Nowhere.* I don't know what motivated her to flip such a crusty booger at me over and over again, until I finally refused to believe those words myself. Maybe she was just trying to run an "end around" on me in some perverse, holistic manner, readying me for the world's mortal blows. Maybe I needed to be told I'd never be anything until I actually tried to be something other than a nobody. I don't know. Maybe some kind of back alley voodoo shit was going on. Maybe my mother was using the same language she grew up with under her own parents. One of which I never met, my grandfather, who died just before I was born. The other being a woman I miss every day of my life, my beautiful and hilarious grandmother, Mary "Mazzy" Mahoney. I don't know how that household worked in Somerville. Maybe, just maybe, she simply didn't know how penetrating her words were and just tried to keep pace with the weekly verbal lashings to temper her wavering mood swings. Then again, maybe hitting me with those jabs, in some twisted way, gave her the edge she needed to make it through another day—to be a wife, a mother, a daughter, a sister, a friend—someone other than who she really wanted to be. I don't know. We never discussed it. And never will.

But those six words she would say, "Who do you think you are?" have dictated my disposition, my drive, my own quest to be heard for as long as I can remember. Forever.

I owe my mother that. And today, I love her for it. All of it.

6. ALL CURLED UP

Thank God my mother welcomed me in because I had nowhere else to go. My father had turned my old bedroom above the garage into his new bedroom while I was away on my tragic sojourn in the North Country. My parent's marriage was running on fumes. Ravaged after 35 years, their union had gone dirty, and the house reeked of anger. Rarely did I see my folks interact, let alone embrace unless either was being gifted something that shined or was framed. And when they needed to occupy the same space around a kitchen sink or a doorway, oh man, it could get chilly. White Walker chilly. Freeze Frame chilly. Snow Miser chilly. A frozen stance of misery flanked with resentment and hostility.

Moving on…

I had no real interest in swimming in the secrets my old bedroom now carried. Something jarring about my middle-aged father crashed out in my old bed, the same bed I slept in when I was 9, 13, 17 and 21. How many raptures must one room endure? If those walls could talk, they would stammer incoherently from a toothless, bleeding mouth. Thinking about my father tucked in the fetal position beneath the covers of my old bed with his hairless legs scratching at my Captain America bedsheets causes my throat to close to this very day. There's just something intensely wrong about it. Then and now.

Years later, and this is true, many nights I would dream about my father dressed in a wrinkled business suit, curled up sleeping in the back seat of his expensive sports car on the side of the road with one door open during the middle of the day. Same dream, night after night.

The finished basement of our home sounded like a perfect place to dismantle this fraud of a life I'd created in those post college years—*Someone, please, just get the wrecking ball. Hoist it high and swing deep. Let the hammer fly. Demolish all that was and was never meant to be.*—After all, my options were nil. I had sacked out on every couch from Allenstown to Woodstock.

Those days had grown old. My antics did too. My friend's nerves were frazzled with my thoughtless acts of destruction—intolerable stuff, like kicking in walls and spilling over cans full of tobacco spit onto carpets covered in beer slime and dead skin.

Once, I was banned from entering a group of friend's rented apartment in Plymouth because I had kicked in one of the bedroom doors in their house one afternoon out of boredom or to scratch the itch which was my ego. The room I barged into was that of a female who lived in the house with my buddies, a young woman I knew and hung out with who didn't appear to have a mean bone in her body. She was quirky, sure, but she was anything but mean. Upon entering the room, I quickly spotted a cream-colored bound notebook that looked, well, it looked like someone's diary, tucked under some magazines and textbooks in a makeshift nightstand made out of milk crates next to the bed. I picked up the book, pondered how I could use this discovery to enhance my funny-guy status among my friends, and then walked back into a living room where a half dozen starch-fat and swollen dudes sat around drinking beer. I proceeded to conduct a brief homily backed by the words of this young woman as I read aloud the beginnings of a very private conversation. Terrible! Appalling! Such a desperate act committed by a wretched, spiteful hack! Something only the ultimate nobody could ever think of doing. I only read a few paragraphs out loud, but that was enough to encase me in a lifetime of shame for what I did. I feel gross and wormy and unworthy of friendship when I recount those days. I did it for laughs, for attention, but I only ended up, likely, humiliating someone much too kind for humiliation.

I wanted to be a heard, to be noticed, to be something. But at what cost?

Regardless of the dirty deed I had done, one thing was certain, I needed out of Chumpsville in the worst kind of way. The bells had tolled. I'd been poisoned by a negative mind. I was infecting the people around me. Everything was about me. Me, me, me, me, me, me. Chasing the applause became an addiction. Corrosive and crass, transparent and petty, it was time to cut the engine, cool the pistons and reevaluate my existence.

Rest stop, please!

7. THE DEAL

My roommate and I packed up what we could into our cars and did the midnight run out of Wellington Hill in Manchester, then we split off our separate ways. We lost all our down payments and probably more in subtle damages, but the flight out of town was a desperate departure from a failed first attempt at adulthood.

I got into my battered 1985 red Dodge and tore ass down 93 south, a broke young man sizzling in defeat. Sunken face and cold to the touch, I rode back into the flatlands of the Bay State, to my hometown of Melrose, returning just as I left it. As a nobody. Exactly where I didn't want to be.

Now what?

My mother, maybe saddened somewhat to witness the unraveling of my worthless trending ways, not only offered me a bed in the basement to sleep in, she offered to pay off the six thousand dollars I owed to the credit card companies. Very generous of her and my father, who, I'm pretty sure, had no idea how screwed I was. And he likely had even less a clue that my mother just wrote a check to Discover Card for six big biscuits. Which was fine with me, because there's a very good chance my father would have squashed the whole deal had he knew what was going on behind the scenes between me and my bookie.

So, my mother and me worked out a payment plan, sans the old man. I happily agreed to kiss the ring. I needed her compassion, but I needed her money more. I could no longer live this way. Anxiety had me by the throat. The deal was, I would pay my mother $100 a month until the tab was paid off. Maybe it was $150 a month, I don't know, but it would be a five-year payment plan. And she triple-dog dared me to miss just one of those payments. She would be relentless if I started dogging her, crazy with rage if I tried to snake my way out of the deal. This I knew. First of the month, no later! That, sonny boy, was the deal. She kept a ledger and she held her word. As did I. Paid in full.

Had my father found out about this black market agreement between me and my mother, I would've been slinging burgers and magic sauce, sporting a netted cap at McDonald's within 24 hours. And I would have been fine with that, because the one thing I vowed to myself as I jetted towards home that late night weeks before with a car full of music cassettes—tapes in the trunk and ten more in the glove compartment, under the seats, on the dash, on my lap, music everywhere—that's when I told myself:

"*Whatever it is you do next, you're not moving for at least two years. You're parking your ass in that seat, on that forklift, behind the wheel of a van or a lawnmower, and you are going to work your way out of this nothingness. You're going to shut your mouth, be on time, duke your mother her monthly nut, and you are going to learn how to be something, someone, anything.*"

That's what I said. And that's what I did.

8. BOBBY MERLOT

Bathed in resentment for nearly 25 years, I started to see, when I moved home, that most of the attacks leveled upon me in my youth by my mother had very little to do with me. The attacks she made were more likely a misdirected hit on her son instead of her wild-eyed, temperamental husband, Robert Sr., otherwise known in some circles as "Bobby Merlot."

The plan, I gather, was for the Azevedo clan to end at three kids, two daughters and a son. Maybe even just two kids, but a Golden Child came out shining at number three. Perfection, my older sister by 18 months, Laura—smart, savvy, beautiful, always in love, always with a plan. In our teens, we would have spit fights around the yard. She would always win, sneaking up around a corner, behind a shrub or car bumper, and dump a lungie on my cheek. Strong, too. Lower body power that developed from years of playing tennis, field hockey and baseball. She threw harder than most dudes. Savvy, as I mentioned, yes indeed. Laura could be an hour late for a presentation, walk in, flash that million-dollar smile and bestow on the staff the real meaning of positivity.

"Now, let's get down to business. I have some ideas about locations to shoot at." Just the best around.

My oldest sister, Lynn, ten years older than me, light years disconnected from action figures and hockey fights, was virtually a stranger to me. For years, I thought she was just a woman that rented a room off the upstairs office in the house. She'd shuffle in the kitchen each morning while I was nursing a bowl of Captain' Crunch at the kitchen table with her magazine beautiful face still pressed with sleep. She'd fill a mug with coffee and cream and I'd study her like I'd study the faces on the train heading into Boston. She kind of looked like me. Maybe she was my aunt on my father's side? Had no clue. I'd finish crunching and slurping and head to the kitchen sink, sauntering my way up next to this beautiful young lady with perfect olive skin and reintroduce myself to her regularly. *"Hi. I'm, ah, I'm . . . Robby."*

With her cup of sugary jet fuel in hand, she'd simply whisper at me as she headed out of the kitchen, a finger pressed to her lips and say, "Shhhh."

My older brother Mike was, well, let's just say, me and Mike didn't hit it off at the git-go. We shared a bedroom, and he is eight years older than me, and holy shit did I bother him until we really connected in my mid-20s. My mere existence from the age of 13 to 25 sent a ferocious amount of anger down his spin. Every night, hours after I had fallen asleep, he would come bounding through the bedroom door and slap on every light in the room, waking me with a halt. Passive aggression at its finest. Then, he would get into bed and flip on the bright lamp that sat on the nightstand dividing our beds and would crack open the latest Philip Roth novel, read for hours, it seemed. Then Mike would turn one eye in my direction with a lip curled like a angry dog before muttering at me, "Shuuuuut up." Real nice and slow.

But four kids, eh, that's not the best setup for a marriage that was slowly unraveling since my father became successful a insurance salesman in the 1980s, years after he stopped delivering office furniture for Jordan Marsh around downtown Boston.

Let me correct myself. My father never "sold insurance." If he heard me mutter those words, man, he would spring from the grave and bust me upside the head with his eyes bugged out, his smokers teeth bent in a hundred directions, seething in his own insecurities. He was a "financial planner," damn it! And that's what he would be referred to as. He was no passionless sales wonk going door to door for a commision check. Not any more he wasn't. No longer did he need to peel apart the wedding announcements in the Sunday Globe, spreading the pages wide open on the living room table and start tracking down all the newlyweds in Massachusetts that yearned for a litter of children. He sold life insurance for years, building his book of clients around Greater Boston and beyond.

My father would scour those pages on Sundays, planning out the phone calls he'd make at first light come Monday morning, lining up sit downs in new little homes with big family dreams where he would remind the beaming newlyweds that yes, life is grand, one big celebration. Enjoy the champagne, for now, until the first door is closed on a life that will impact many other lives. *"These are people you love, and if you plan to keep anything in the trough for the kids when you, God forbid, someone happens to kick off shoveling snow at the mouth of the driveway after another dreadful February storm, you want to have a backup plan, kids."* Blah, blah,

blah. You know the pitch. Even if my father didn't frame it that way, which of course he didn't, or maybe he did, we've all bought into the fear.

You didn't really want to get into with my father. At least I didn't. He scared the hell out of me growing up. If his fuse got lit, forget it. Blast off! A shit storm of trouble was coming.

Never much of a drinker (until he was), my father was more of a loner, a guy that might crack open a Miller Lite on a Sunday afternoon, then sip at it a few times as he watched his beloved New England Patriots pound it out on the gridiron. Then, later, that same warm, three-quarter full can of Miller Lite would be placed back into the refrigerator and nibbled at all week long, flat as all fuck. Until the next Sunday came around and my father would polish off what was left of the old swill at the bottom of the can, then pop another beer before stretching it out another seven days. That was maybe the strangest thing my father did on a regular basis. That, and shitting in the dark at night with the bathroom door wide open, smoking a copious amount of Barclay cigarettes.

If my father knew about the financial agreement between my mother and me, my Dad would've verbally castrated both of us, likely ending with me huddled in some corner sobbing about being a "nothing." Whiny little twit. GET UP! BE A MAN! DO SOMETHING! He would never have thrown me out of the house, though. He was too much of a softy on the inside, knowing exactly what it feels like to be banished.

For some odd reason, when my father was a child, his parents would send him away every summer to a town called Malden, a simple six miles from his bedroom in Cambridge. I don't know who he lived with during those months, maybe a distant aunt or some shit, a cousin. And I don't remember hearing about my grandparents taking any seasonal retreats to the Alps or the Catskills during the summer. Humberto, my grandfather, was a barber in South Boston for years at a shop called Murphy's. My gramps didn't have a stitch of Irish in him. He was fresh off the boat from the Azores, I think. I don't remember him ever really talking at all, just whistling all the time and dressed to the nines—shoes, hat, pressed jacket. My grandmother, Rose, was a yeller, a loud, passionate Portuguese woman that rarely, if ever, roamed far from her tenement in Cambridge. But for some strange reason, Malden was where my father spent his summers, basking in the all the wonders of Malden, pizza joints and car washes.

And that's why my father would never have kicked me out of the house.

9. DUST BALL BLUES

My father was gone, I think, soon after I moved back home. He was roughing it out somewhere on the North Shore, getting a little bit more lonelier day-by-day living the bachelor life. I stayed with him just one night, crashing out on his couch in a nearly-empty apartment on a quiet street in Peabody. A harrowing experience to witness either parent as a broken human being. Never leaves you. And Good Christ, this was ugly.

Unpolished and uncommonly reckless, my father was living just as I was only months before, literally, it seemed. No food in the house, ashtrays everywhere, sleepless nights with dreams so far from being realized you'd need a scanner to find it. Half-filled glasses of water gone gray were scattered on the kitchen counters. There was a stink to the place that smelled of death, of loneliness, like a rotten open sore. Nothing had ever been cooked on the stove, or so it appeared. Rumor has it, my father was seen dumping buckets of water from the kitchen sink into the washing machine, trying to get his whites clean. Having never done laundry a day in his life, or at least since his younger days as Marine, my father, at 55, was dead on the line, cursing that damn spin cycle.

That was the last time I ever slept under the same roof as my father. The next morning, I awoke from a series of nightmares, all clammy with sweat from tossing and turning on my father's jagged couch. The first thing I saw when I got my bearings was a handful of dust balls floating around under a coffee table in the living room. Airless, the dust balls looked lost, aimless, meandering towards nothing.

The second thing I saw was my father, pale and not as physically tight as I remember him being, dressed only in his underwear, which actually looked a few spins cycles short of clean. He was making a pot of coffee and smoking his first butt of the day. Not too long before this glorious morning, my father was a swimmer and he played tennis regularly when he was in his 30s and 40s. He was never cut like an adonis. He was build more like, well, let's see now, like, like, like Don Draper! Yes, like the actor. Asymmetrical and definitely one of the "Mad Men."

But on this morning, when the sky seemed flat and gray—hopeless even—as he drained his first cup of coffee, cranking away at a smoke, my father looked like I did then: skinny, loose and disconnected from the rest of the world. His lean muscles had gone flat. His skin ashen. He was unkempt, and there was a sadness in the eyes that hurt to stare into.

So, instead of intensifying this dismal turn of events, instead of adding to the nauseas setting, I thanked my father for letting me crash on his couch and I crawled my way back home.

One and done rooming with my father.

10. DAD DIED BROKE

Years later, my Dad died broke. We never knew he was broke until, well, until we knew. By "we" I mean my brother and sisters. This revelation presented itself just two months before that pig-faced monster—otherwise known as cancer—put an end to him for good in 2011, at the age of 70.

I still can't muster up the guts to delete his number from my cell phone. Ah, so be it.

When you're watching a parent die, or anyone, young, old or ancient die—as my dear retired neighbor Hank was watching his wife of 35 years die before his eyes—the horror is all you can focus on.

For awhile.

Sooner or later the bill comes calling and she's equally ugly as the pig face. And just as big a priority. Numbers stacked on procedures, on lab runs, on ambulances to only deepen the fear and toil.

Real scary stuff.

When we learned my father had virtually nothing left to his name in the form of property or finances when he died, we were shocked. We knew he wasn't "well off" anymore.

The 1980s was a wonderful time for making money if you didn't mind the hustle. My Dad hustled. Worked his way off a furniture truck to be a country-club-card carrying cranky pants with a long-time financial business in downtown Melrose, Mass.

He drove a BMW, bought a big brick house, spent little on himself, had few friends, smoked a lot of butts and read a lot of books. He was a success! All this by age 50. Not bad.

And my neighbor, Hank, the one who was losing his wife, was a successful too. IIe got early retirement like a 100 years ago from the phone company, in his early 50s. Best health plan ever. Best pension. Best place in the world to be let go, back then anyways.

Hank figured he was covered financially. He was wrong.

I can remember on countless occasions, looking over at Hank messing around in his yard like a happy dog on some fine Monday morning—mowing, clipping, washing—and thinking to myself, "Now I want to be him instead of the cat."

Then, one night, Hank arrives at my back door in tears. At a loss, this old man, so strong, hands like horse saddles, was busted up like no one's business. His mouth was quivering, buckets of tears beyond his thick glasses. He's telling how his wife said before she died, "Goodbye. You've been a good man, a good husband."

Then Hank starts talking about his life, all the years he worked, the money he saved, the Golden years he was promised. "Not-so-golden…." Yeah, I know that one, too.

He's angry and terrified as he should be about the mounting bills. No person past their 70s should suffer going broke, that's a young man's game. But millions of seniors are drowning in debt, trying to heat their homes, pay for medications, eat some food and keep their butts out of the retirement home, where they'll absolutely go broke.

Brutal business, this life thing.

Prophetic in hiding his financial demise, of course out of pride and shame, my father, amazingly, found himself so underwater that he stopped fighting against the current. He retired too early at 53. Stopped hustling and dreamed too big.

With earning out of the equation, every buck he borrowed and spent led him deeper into the abyss. Had we children had an inkling he was drowning in something other than that pig-faced monster's own slobber, we could have helped. But the Christmas cards with cash inside arrived each year for the grandkids. Weddings and dinners were paid for, colleges funded, credit extended.

He seemed comfortable, safe. I always thought he was being shrewd with his finances, in a survival sort of way. Live on the cheap, bare-boned but not busted. Spend it all but make it last.

Impossible these days.

As one finance friend of mine told me, "You have no idea how broke so many people your father's age are. And you would never know it."

But my old man was no street urchin thumbing for nickels on a cold winter's night. And neither is Hank. Nobody should live that way, under a guise of ease and stability when in actuality the pig face isn't only chowing down on your life line, but on your pride, sanity and Golden Years.

Wish I had a better perspective, but the pig face ate that too.

11. THE EPITOME OF MEDIOCRITY

All teeth and lips with a set of flaring nostrils built out of an oily mix of Portuguese and Irish descent, I was a frightened, skinny kid who had it all growing up in Melrose, a small city just eight miles north of Boston.

Country club dilettante.

Worse than average student.

B-league tennis star.

Breaststroke alternate on the club swim team.

Backyard baseball player.

No speed, weak arm, all talk, a showoff.

The epitome of mediocrity.

Ok, sure, I was all that. I had no game, no spirited friendships, just people who put up with me. I had some skills as an athlete but never enough to be truly relevant. I could carry myself on a basketball court and baseball field, but rarely made an impact on a game. I played one down of varsity football in high school for the Red Raiders, but then was immediately pulled from the field for a "late hit" and never saw action again. I hit the opposing receiver hard as fuck, and late on purpose. Drove my shoulder pad right up under his helmet. Cheap shot. I figured back then, any reaction was better than no reaction. And I got a reaction, just not from the grandstands. Unimpressed with my nothingness, the only shouting I heard came from the coaches on the sidelines, screaming, "You! Number 20! Get off the field!"

Not a single roar from crowd.

I had friends but none of them really truly liked me. Tolerated me mostly. Can't blame them. I was bullish and cruel, capable of ringing the life out of any relationship. I'd burn them to the ground by trying to downsize them, cutting them down to swim in the same steamy pot of misery I had cooking for myself . And for what reasons? Fear and insecurity, I suppose. Of what? Who really knows. Too scared to find out. Too cheap to ask.

But within that nothingness, I was the ultimate daydreamer, wrapped up in fantasy to this very day. I would play for hours in my manicured backyard wearing shiny cowboy boots and black leather women's gloves pretending I was Nick Barkley from *The Big Valley*. You remember him, don't you? The black angel brother of "Heath Barkley," the illegitimate son played by Lee Majors. I'd cut the fingers off my baseball batters gloves and wear a tough guy scally cap backwards on my head and think I was Sly Stallone from 1981 when he played a NYC police detective alongside Billie Dee Williams in "*Night Hawks*."

In the finished basement of our home, there was a brick fireplace, a large Zenith television, some stereo equipment, a couch with a long mirror over it and one massive, mustard yellow pillow covered in corduroy. The pillow must have weighed 20-pounds, or so it seemed. And that pillow and me, well, we battled whenever there was Boston Bruins game broadcasting out of Boston on WSBK TV 38. Those were the days of the brawling Bruins, with Jay Miller and Chris Nilan, Stan Jonathan and Cam Neely, all capable of caving in the side of an opponent's head with a series of crushing blows to the helmet and jawbone.

Round and round me and that pillow would go when a ice brawl broke out between teams. My small hands would rain haymakers down on the top of that pillow right where the thick zipper stretched across the top, holding in the foam. If my knuckles weren't bleeding and my tee-shirt was still intact, then it must have been a weak-ass fight between the clubs. Maybe even just a two-minute misconduct. But if the benches cleared and even the goalies were sprinting the length of the ice to throttle one another with the waffle gloves, then I would nearly break my own nose by repeatedly slamming my face into the pillow, purposely making my nose and lips bleed. Fucking into it!

I would land blow after blow on the ribs of the pillow. I'd tackle it, one arm it into the corner of the couch before charging that pillow like a fight dog at a snake hunt. Then, just as the hockey players were separated and finally crammed into the penalty boxes, adjusting their elbow pads and spitting blood at the ice, I'd look up with pride at my own blood-stained buck teeth, my red cheeks, my watery eyes in the long mirror and feel like something, someone. Anything but a nobody.

12. WRAPPED IN FANTASY

Wrapped up in fantasy, yes, that's what I was. All day, anytime I could get it. In my basement toy room, I wasn't so much conducting seminars on the Art of Nerf Basketball, but creating a world around it, a league with rules and stats and standings that didn't even exist. Indeed, the level of punishment I administered upon myself when I'd slam my stick-thin frame against the panelled wall going for an offensive rebound was pretty heroic. Shaq himself could not have contained me. The dunks, indescribable. Chocolate Thunder and Dominique Wilkins all rolled into one. Finger rolls that dripped with butter. Shooting clinics of Hall of Fame caliber were conducted from behind a toy chest, George "Iceman" Gervin style.

Last second winning shots spawned rally cries from the kitchen where my mother would be cooking up a feast for the 5:30 dinner hour. "Knock it off down there, you eggitt!" she would screech down the basement stairs just as I was about to hit a buzzer beater. *"Knock it off? Knock it off? Woman, I got a nail biter going on down here! Kiki just fouled out! McHale's at the line!"* That's what I wanted to say. But I didn't, of course. Instead, I'd run into the next room, the fight room, where the mustard pillow rested beaten between a chair and a coffee table, stained with kid blood and loose to the touch. I'd faceplant myself right into the pillow and start wailing away at it, as if a full-on-brawl broke out at half court between Dr. J, Larry Bird and that coward Moses Malone, who dared to choke Larry Legend from behind in 1984 as Julius Erving teed off on Bird's face.

In my bedroom, rarely would you find me belly down on the bed with my feet tangled and wagging behind me as I read what I was suppose to be reading for school. I'd be on the floor instead playing with my action figures, full on toy soldiers spitting wind and sand around the desert lands of North Africa fighting off those Nazi's hogs in jeeps mounted with 50-caliber machine guns.

"Rat Patrol" style.

These moments often saved me. To be lost in a mind sweep of possibility and adventure was a deep cleanse to me, a blanket I could escape under where the truth wasn't allowed in. Nut Jobs Only! But sooner than not, I'd be called away from my fantasyland and led back to the legion of doom where everything sucked. I sucked, you sucked, she sucked, school sucked, the town sucked, everything sucked because nothing seemed to matter. Certainly not me.

13. THINGS HAVE CHANGED

But then in August 1977, things changed. The King died. *Elvis Presley* himself. And at seven years old, I had no clue who Elvis Presley was. But when the Boston Globe arrived to our home the week he died, I remember picking through the remains of the paper after my father and older brother, Mike, tore through the metro region, sports, travel and editorial sections like two animals tugging at the same side of beef.

Somewhere inside the cartoon section and mixed in with a hundred coupon cutouts from various grocery stores, I came across a 11x17-inch picture of this guy from Memphis named Elvis. He was sweaty, jowly, tanned and fucking marvelous. My God, he was magnetic, a cannon of light sent to me by, yes, the gods. Who else could it have been that tapped me on the shoulder with this vision and said, "Don't let this moment get away, little buddy. Grab it. It just might be what saves you."

The background of the picture was black, but the image of Elvis was a live shot from a concert and definitely not taken during his reign as a young, thin-hipped sex machine that dampened many a virgin's jeans from here to Abilene. He was gripping a microphone, thick fingers dressed in silver and gold diamonds. The cuff on his wrists were turned up ballroom fancy. Heavy chains around his neck, of course. The left hand corner of the picture was saved for the lyrics from his famous song "Love Me Tender."

Love me tender, love me sweet,
Never let me go.
You have made my life complete,
And I love you so.

Love me tender, love me true,
All my dreams fulfill.
For my darlin', I love you,
And I always will.

This was the moment I'd been waiting for. Someone telling me there was more to all this living than just nothing. I might still be nothing, but this guy Elvis was certainly something. And his something was rubbing off on me, right through my eyes, my skin, my heart. Up and away his spirit flew around me, inside me. Wordless hymns of a new beginnings swam in my head. I had found my Reason to Believe. All because of this very simply picture paying tribute to a dead rock and roll pioneer.

Bob Dylan wrote in a passage from his autobiography *Chronicles* about an epiphany he had years after losing faith in his own abilities as a writer and performer in the late 1980s. He said, "Instantly, everything came back like a thoroughbred had charged through the gates. Everything came back, and came back in multidimensions."

Dylan was on tour with Tom Petty and the Heartbreakers and basically mailing it in, passionless and disconnected from the legendary lyrics he wrote in the 1960s and 70s behind such great songs as "Like A Rolling Stone" "Isis" and "Tangled Up in Blue." Until one night when he was rehearsing for a few tour dates with the Grateful Dead in San Francisco, a breakthrough occurred. Again, Dylan was going through the motions, he said, unwilling to invest much effort in the very songs that made him an icon. The Dead wanted to basically go through nearly the entire catalogue of Dylan songs, the rarities, sleepers and hits. Dylan just wanted to play the same songs he'd been playing with the Heartbreakers. In-and-out, get on home. He ended up leaving the studio alone that night and just started walking the streets of San Fran. Rain was coming down and he ducked into a small bar where he heard some jazz being played. The joint was virtually empty but the music being played by the small four piece band was "unpredictable" and transformative, taking Dylan back to a time when risk and feel played a vital role in creating the musician he actually was.

This is what Elvis did to me. It woke me from a slumber I didn't know I was living in.

Bam, I was alive!

14. NOTHING BUT THE MUSIC

After that extraordinary awakening finding the picture of Elvis in the paper, it was time to raid the record collections of my parents, my brothers, my neighbors, and get my hands on the message of Elvis. I had a record player in my bedroom but I never used it. I was too busy battling it out in the desert sands with my action figures to look up and consider playing any music out of it. Didn't seem to matter.

Then it did. And by the the time I bought or stole or was given "Pure Gold" by Elvis Presley, I was locked into a world that forty years later still provides me with the courage, the will, the mission behind my own quest to be heard. Music.

"Pure Gold" led to another by Elvis, "C'mon Everybody" (a song by Elvis I still sing in the shower) which led to the group Sha Na Na, Bowzer, The Fonz, Rocky Balboa, and then Pony-Boy from the "Outsiders." Then, a little later down the road, the Jersey Flash himself, Mr. Bruce Springsteen took over my life, literally. Those were my cabinet members, my acting saviors, each personality slowly filling in a gaping hole of nothingness, melding together an attitude, a lifestyle, a passion, a wholly different conversation that would slowly burn throughout four decades of development.

My brother, Mike, was mad about his music. He'd lock himself downstairs in the fight room for hours cranking Jackson Browne, Leo Sayer and a whole lotta James Taylor. We didn't communicate much in those days, him in high school, me, eight years younger, just a knot of nerves with nothing to say. But telepathy entered in through the music, and I grew as he grew because the music he played downstairs, well, he didn't hold back on the volume. Seemingly always there, before school and after, cutting through the gloom and good times on Sherwood Road, the music Mike played reached me in ways that still influences me today.

The simple beats, the heavy thinking wordplay, the triumphant hero leveled by a life less given. These songs filled me with a kind of sorrow that I wanted to drink in, feeding me in ways that didn't require a textbook or instruction by some equally unnerved individual with a hint of narcissism. There was much more to this music than just listening to it. It was a subculture, a new way of thinking where you didn't ask for approval any longer. You stole your identity, you made it up, you took it for yourself because nobody was going to knock on your front door and hand it to you. The pump, the emotion, the life force within all that music is what kept the wolves at bay for me.

One time I came home from school having been called "Rudolph" by nearly every asshole that passed me in the halls. A day earlier I'd tried to lance a zip on my nose using a threading needle and a heavy splash of Brut Aftershave and ending up with a massive bleeding welt on the tip of my nose that lasted for weeks. The teasing I had to withstand was monumental, a mad force of cruelty. Still, the ribbing was bearable. "Rail on dickheads," I said to myself. I'd endured worse ridicule in my own home.

Nothing could reach me. Nothing but the music.

In the kitchen, as I tiptoed around my mother reaching for a bag of cold cuts and a tub of mayo in the fridge, the music my brother played that crashed through the basement door was never Top 40. Not progressive rock or metal either. Mike liked mostly singer songwriters. Like many of the ones from all around New Hampshire that I get to interview each week on my radio show "Granite State of Mind."

Jackson Browne was smart, but a little too casual for me. His wordage was spot on, especially when I ingested hours of listening to one of my favorites by him, "Lives in the Balance." Still, he just wasn't a "deserted on an island" must. Leo Sayer was a party, a spectacle of sorts that inspired you to not give a fuck what others think. Just dance! Crank it up! And brother James Taylor with his long smooth fingers and perfect nasal pitch made me think of a home I didn't know existed in Massachusetts.

Fire, rain, love, all of it shot up from the fight room where Mike played the music of his life, the music that raised him up and separated him from the masses. I liked his approach to beating back the belittlement we, at times, endured at home, so I adopted it. And although at the time Mike didn't much like me outside of the required love part, we had this silent understanding that music was the only way out of this emotional mess we lived in.

Degradation, manipulation, intimidation, they couldn't touch us, not when the music was busy pumping hope and promise in our veins. Let that music, all those images, all those power chords and ballads, let them play heavy on your mind. This is what I told myself. Tenderness, anger, abandonment, all the classic themes of rock and roll, let them rattle inside your head, your heart, your mind, because they are there for a reason. Believe it.

Never a season went by without Mike's music shifting the balance of my growth. Through the cigarette smoke coming from the den where my father, clad in a bathrobe and bed pants, sat reading a mystery novel or something in the paper, it was Dan Fogelberg during the winters and hot summers spent listening to this guy named Bruce growl his way through the Darkness on the Edge of Town.

By that point, I was a teen and well on my way to accepting this trumped up quest of mine, this thirst to be heard somehow, someway. Oh, I had no plan. I wasn't ever going to learn how to play guitar. Wasn't in the cards or the fingers for me. The only fret I knew was generated by my parents, and the only chord I ever considered was the one I would wrap around my neck when all this nothingness finally grew into something ugly one day. I couldn't sing, couldn't write, couldn't get a word out without spitting a lisp. But this growth I speak of needed to be fed and fed often in order to be revealed. No longer could I depend solely on my brother's music to free me from this state of nothingness. Indeed, his passions shook the chains, weakened the drive link, but it wasn't *my* trip. It was *his* trip. And, in order to deliver on this self-imposed quest to heard, I would need to believe not just in the music, but in myself.

15. STAIRWAY TO HEAVEN

So long, cowboy boots. The action figures went in the closet. Enough of that shit. Now, I just needed a train pass that would take me from Oak Grove Station in Malden, Mass. right into Downtown Crossing in Boston, where through the stink of hot piss and a thousand different faces, I would double step my way up the heavy stairs that led out onto Washington Street, where just a few clicks up on Winter Street. stood the patron saint of record stores: "Stairway to Heaven."

This place was my library, my Sistine Chapel, my own personal time machine that would transport me from out of the gloomy tensions within my life and catapulte me into a world of cool. Posters, books, records, tapes, cassettes, pins, magnets, magazines, bumper stickers, rock patches for denim jackets. It was an explosion of individuality, a reckoning, a paradise of lust, confusion and a fair amount of buried rage. I would hang out there for hours at least once or twice a month, fingering through the 45's, searching and searching for those rare B-sides I'd been reading about in my older brother's subscription to *Rolling Stone*.

You could smell the vendor meat cooking greasy hot on the streets as you pushed your way through a stack of "Abba" albums. The girls wearing dark mascara and black lipstick kicking around in army boots and ripped fishnet stockings were actually strolling the same aisles I was. Imagine that! They looked nothing like the well groomed Polo wearing female friends of mine from home, who were bright and beautiful, no doubt, but never dangerous. Exotic and unreachable, my young loins ached to sample the smooth necks of these toughies and light their cheap cigarettes as they purified or decimated the greatness of The Clash, The Police, The Cars, Ozzy or Aerosmith.

The ghost-faced and pudgy progressive cats that worked the registers and pledged allegiance to The Smiths, Brian Eno, Rush and King Crimson, were scary in their own right. Stone cold rock fanatics. Historians of punk.

Metal messiahs. You wouldn't have four words out of your mouth, ready to ask the guy stacking the New Releases with a label gun in hand, *"Hey, do you know where..."* before a wagging finger would silently direct you towards a corner of the store built for my sensibilities.

How did he know I was looking for a copy of "Hot August Nights?"

These characters, mostly men, as I remember it, inspired me to step out of my own cage. Why? I haven't a clue worth spit. Just because. Their intelligence, draped behind the cozy confines of resistance, and their cagey looks, their tired eyes, I don't know what it was about them, about the store, how it smelled cluttered but at the same time was filled with nothing. The place seemed to have boobie trapped my mind until I had fresh tracks ready to be built upon. Even when the cashiers rolled their eyes at me when I'd drop a Johnny Cougar record on the counter and they'd give me that—"What is this shit?"—dirty ass look, I was fine with it. I trusted them. At least they noticed me. My music. My tastes. Something stood out. Something more than nothing.

The Greaseheads in their vintage Zeppelin concert tee shirts and rusty high-top sneakers bent at the sides with the tongues hanging out were busy buying cassettes for their wrecks outside. They seemed to step right off the big screen to me. Shit yeah, just like on Springsteen's "Backstreets." They smelled of sweat and smoke and exuded an attitude that bordered on criminal. Aggressive and probably overlooked, kneeling towards the dark side of the road with their ciggy teeth and flat eyes, these cats I couldn't exactly relate to, but that never stopped me from wanting to be kind of just like them. No way, I said. They were Nick Barkley smoking bonsai weed. Even if I was only a 13-year-old spoiled rich kid from the toney streets of Melrose, basting in my own sense of entitlement, I could hear the cries of these dark angels screaming to be seen or simply just recognized.

Just like me.

But, I hadn't reached their level of disenchantment yet. I was still a pretty boy in ironed jeans playing rock star in my bedroom with a wooden tennis racket, singing into a Orange Crush soda can. But, standing in that stairway, staring into this sea of creativity, wishing it was really what heaven looked like, I couldn't help but feel some semblance of steel forming in my spine. When I'd be searching the hundreds of racks for the very music that would ultimately define me, I felt a sense of understanding, of community, of acceptance in that record store. I can't explain it. But I loved it.

I went to Stairway to Heaven as often as my parents let me. Which was pretty often because at some point in my teens, life was just better when I was out of the house. Not just for them, but for me. A blanket of negativity engulfed me at home. It was in my hair, my skin, the souls of my keepers. I couldn't do right by them, and I wasn't giving them much a reason to pronounce me as a good son. I was alright, but I was a moody little bitch. Still am. Moving on.

My father, as I said, mostly scared the shit out of me. Too unpredictable, too much like myself. My mother was mostly on edge and seemingly ready to pounce at the slightest infraction. Dishes in the sink, shoes on the rugs, clothes on the floor. You would have thought I took down Babylon.

"Who do you think you are?"

Still nobody, Ma. (Psst….but I'm gaining ground, woman. I can feel it.)

16. TAKING OFF

Typing class, 1983. The whole classroom smelled of mouth and cigarettes, rank ones at that. Long Winston 100s probably. Mrs. Mahoney liked her smokes. And I liked Mrs. Mahoney, everyone did. She was a big personality around the school, that rare teacher nobody minded getting assigned to. Her classes were like a buoy offshore that you swam towards when the waves in English or science class started turning over on you. She was positive, steady at her craft and extremely kind. Her voice had a deep timbre to it, deeper than most of the fathers of the kids she taught the hunt and peck or hybrid style of typing to. She also had a particular scent, that of an older aunt who comes to your home for a holiday and tries to cover up her dirty habits with a heavy splash of Jean Nate.

I can smell her right now. It's comforting.

I didn't daydream about napping with Mrs. Mahoney like I did some of my first few teachers. Maybe because she had the same last name as my own mother when my mother was still a Mahoney. I don't think it was that though. I never knew my mother as a Mahoney, so it was probably because I just wasn't attracted to Mrs. Mahoney like I was, say, Mrs. Travers, who, in my childish mind, was busy being married to my hero, the Six Million Dollar Man (again, Lee Majors) when she wasn't teaching me about the elements of storytelling in the third grade.

She wore the most spectacular moon-colored blouses and her skin was coca-butter smooth.

Typing was a struggle at first. Hitting the keys precisely where they were meant to be hit for a fat-fingered freak like me, you'd think I would have aced it. These mitts can cover some ground. Not on the Royal keys though, not often enough. I'd hit the "R" and end up stroking the "T" I'd try to pinky finger the "L" and end up sending the return lever flying. I was all over the place. White Out City. Mrs. Mahoney would lean over my desk with a hand on my shoulder, her hot breath on my neck, and tell me to slow down, use every finger, get a feel for the keys, use a balanced touch. "Concentrate, Robby. Stop rushing." Rushing towards what?

Balance was something I desperately needed in typing class and in life. Again, I was all over the place, like many kids in their early teens. I couldn't figure out why I had a stomach ache most of the day, every day. Nervous nearly all the time, a wrack of bones with a nose that shined like a midnight carpet bombing, I was desperately trying to fit in. Too hard, probably. Witless and without a plan, I conducted my days leaning in on most conversations. I didn't have much to say myself, so I'd always saddle up next to one of the funnier guys in the school and laughed a little louder than everyone else when someone's balls were getting properly busted.

I also found that having a solid baseball card collection was crucial in my social development. Error cards were a big thing back then, baseball cards that were printed with some obvious flaw, like the 1979 Bump Wills card that features the right-handed journeyman infielder wearing a Texas Ranger uniform, but the front of the card read: BLUE JAYS. That's gold in the trading card world, even if it only goes for a few bucks on the market. I owned it. Then lost it. Stupid.

At some point during that year in typing class, a group of four guys formed in the back of the typing class. I was one of them. Three months into the class, most of us had the gist of typing down, hovering somewhere around 66 words per minute. I found the exercise to be a pain in the ass, personally. I recognized long before ever seeing a computer that whatever form of efficiency this was—it was failing. Between the constant ribbons twists and the keys ripping into the sides of my ink stained fin gernails, I was fully annoyed. The others were, too. Cliffy Mac and Magic, Magoo and myself, we were sore from pounding out our assignments, which didn't take terribly long, usually leaving us with a good twenty minutes to tell lies to each other before the class ended.

Towards the end of one of these classes, someone suggested we each write a column about the more notable sports figures at our school, a very watered-down one-page grammatically challenged sports column. The other three members of this trumped-up sports department were already leading men at our school for their terrific athletic prowess. Cliff

McDonald was a powerhouse wrestler and football player. Later he went on and played linebacker at Dartmouth College. Whip smart, too. Chad McGuire was a gunslinger as a quarterback at Melrose for the Red Raiders, and he could dish and dash as hoop player. Handsome to the core. Derek Maggicomo was the "do anything" kid. Hit a liner in the gap with the game tied in the ninth, or drive to the bucket, get whacked and knock down both shots at the free-throw line. He did all that and managed to be one of the nicest guys in town. That was Magic.

We were all fans of sportscaster, Bob Lobel, on Boston's WBZ-TV Channel 4. He had a show called Sports Final back in the 80s that ran once a week on Sundays and it was hit. Between the hilarious blooper reels that featured the best "worst" moments in sports that week, Lobel conducted some fantastic, deep-cut interviews with players from the Boston Celtic, the Patriots, Bruins and the Red Sox, who you loved to watch play the game but never heard speak a phrase. You can see that same format played daily on 500 channels these days. But back then, Lobel, with his gentle swag and good-buddy manner, would sit down with these titans of the game and the viewers would learn a thing or two about the players that made us dream of being a hero, just once.

So, away we went, ready to draft the one and only sports column ever written in Mrs. Mahoney's typing class. We all had titles ready to go, that was the easy part. "Cliff's Corner," Magic's Moments," "The Big Magoo." I called mine, "Aza's Sports Final," going for what was already working for the successful commentator, Mr. Lobel, a man who had no problem draping himself in fur. I figured, if it works for Bobby, it works for me. Maybe I could grab me some of those high ratings.

There was heat on my chest, in my wrists, my arms, as I started writing my first-ever "published" lines. Something was connecting within my hands and my brain that I never felt before. I didn't think about it, I just did it. I simply started having an internal conversation with myself where I was both the interviewer and the subject, writing about things that I could only assume others were interested in reading.

Being so long ago, I can't remember exactly what I wrote that day, but for the most part, it was strictly conversational. About three paragraphs, a mere 250 words. The tone I adopted was that of a hard-boiled city columnist chewing down on a soggy cigar at deadline. I was going for the kill, for blood, for a ring I had never worn before. I wanted this to work. No idea why. I just wanted to kill this column.

With so few grudges in those days, much of that having to do with my flaccid social life, I basically started roasting some of my peers, the ones who could handle—and deserved—a solid roasting. I wasn't gunning for the geeks and twinks. I was circling the Big Game, the student athletes with the meatiest hides, thick with bone and horn. I had my focus points, my reasons to hassle. Picking out a football player and waxing on about his nauseating, self-congratulating manner was a risky move, no doubt. But it had to be done. The chances of me taking a beating behind a grocery store by a brawny leatherneck with movie-star looks were excellent. But I was willing to take a whooping in order to be noticed, to be heard.

Like a death sentence overturned, I leapt inside, feeling brand new. Alive! I started cutting and slashing sentences, trying to make the words dance, make them sing, bring them to life. My blood thinned as hot oil ran out of my fingertips. I was in a zone, a meditative state, like I was "chasing white lines." I blocked everyone out around me, even when I heard the other guys asking over my shoulder, "What are you writing about, guy? You look possessed." I never looked up or responded to their inquiries because my mind was on fire as I tried to keep pace with my head and my hands. A mad sprint ensued. I have to finish this column!

We had twenty minutes to construct these pieces and then, poof, just like that, I knew that this foray into the publishing world would have ended, probably forever. Tomorrow, a new idea would emerge within the group and the sport department would have been disbanded. For what? A comedy troupe? A rock band? A break-dancing crew? There was no tomorrow, there was just today, for me at least. I was the only one in the group who had any real skin in the game. Like I said, the other guys were bonafide superstars in school, like Sammy, Frank and Dean, all rolled into one. Long established, fat with flash, they were cool while I was a lippy slave to the emotional grind. I yearned for some of that noticeability that greased the tracks of their existence. Fuck, yeah!

The bell rang and you're damn right I finished. Panting, I ripped that paper out of the roller and held it high, as if showing off my byline in the editorial section of the "Sunday New York Times." The other three guys didn't scratch much out with their columns. Couple words here, a sentence there. No commitment, just a few gags. I understood why. What's the point? Lebron James doesn't write about Lebron James. Other people do that.

Walking out of class and into the crowded halls, one of the guys grabbed the piece of paper out of my hand and immediately started laughing at something I wrote. Then, one of the other guys took it and read a line and laughed. "Wait a minutes, who you calling..." My back grew wings with every chuckle that arose out of my friends. They were loving my shit! *My* shit!

Shouldering our way through the halls, ready to separate to our next classes, I tugged at my buddy, wanting the column back. But it was gone, dashed off into the hands of someone else to be misunderstood or offended or entertained, or, more likely, found on the ground inside the boys bathroom, urine soaked and disowned.

"Damn," I thought to myself . "I worked hard on that thing. I want it back. I want to read it again."

I soon resigned myself and went on with my day. OK, time to get back to anonymity. That was fun though, I thought, and what a rush, better than every breast I never got to touch or see in those days. Not planning a follow-up piece on the state of athletics at Melrose High school, I figured, it was time to return to my constant state of nothingness. It was ok, I had got used to it.

And then, just like that, out of nowhere, someone came up to me in the cafeteria during lunch and said, "Hey, Az, I just read that thing you wrote. It was pretty fuckin' funny." Then after lunch, someone else I didn't usually talk to said pretty much the same thing. "Funny shit, Az. Ya, that kid is a dick." This was fantastic. I was elated, besides myself. It's what I wanted, needed. We all have needs and that was mine. I needed to know something was out there for me. Something more than nothing. Anything but nothing, and I found it. Whatever happened within the twenty minutes that I wrote that column was now meant to be acted upon. This I knew. How did I know? I don't know. I just knew. And, I wanted to keep that feeling going.

One more comment in the hall and perhaps a few dirty looks later, and that was that. My day of glory was over. It would take me nearly ten years before I'd write my next column. But I always looked back on that day in Mrs. Mahoney's typing class as The Day, as one of those pinnacle moments when you realize some dreams are worth suffering over.

17. THE OUTSIDER

I had no idea where to start or how to cultivate this new obsession of mine, writing. It wasn't like I took to a fountain pen and began cranking out stories about lost youth and internal crisis on legal pads under candlelight in my bedroom. Please. I would have done just that if I had thought of it, but I never did. I pretty much just hung onto that one day in Mrs. Mahoney's typing class and rode that memory of being something more than nothing for nearly ten years.

Sounds obscene and manic, I know. I get that. I am both those things. But I did more than just loiter on the images of that day. I wanted to get that feeling back. It was intoxicating, the nods of approval, the flattery. Yet, it was so much more than just a slow hand job. There was meaning within the whispers of those words, a clear message from beyond. Yuck, right? I know, it all sounds very Oprahish, but that's just how it goes, baby. An opportunity presented itself—visually, spiritually, physically—and I chose to grab it with both hands instead of just pissing it away. Like I had done countless times before.

But I also knew that the brew wasn't ready to sip just yet. My jive still needed time to percolate, to gather steam before being served up again. I had to think big about the days ahead. This was no casual encounter with fate. This was fate grabbing me by the face, scratching my balls, tickling my ears, shouting, "Take me, you dumb shit!"

So, I reworked that mother of a memory and turned it over in my head for nearly a decade, creating a personality and a voice behind the meager 250 words I had written, trying to scratch out some kind of formula to get it all back again someday. Or fuck all!

I loved baseball as a kid, still do. And I knew that like a pitcher on a baseball team, in order for them to learn how to throw a slow breaking ball, a slider or sinker, they needed to study the craft, endlessly, figure out angles and trajectory, speed and range. And do it over and over again thousands of times. You can be born with talent, but anything born needs feeding. And that's where books came into the picture for me. I needed to feed my face full of literature, words, voices, characters and box scores. I needed to shake the rust off my insatiably horny teenage brain and get cracking on some books.

And then, BAM! Just like that, S.E. Hinton came into my life, the great writer of teenage classics like "The Outsiders," " Rumble Fish" and "That Was Then This is Now." We were assigned The Outsiders in English class sometime soon after my Grand Day and I immediately grimaced at the thought of actually reading a book straight through. I had done it before, sure, but I mostly faked it. My grades proved that.

"What is this shit now?" I'm sure I said myself when Hinton's book came sliding cross my desktop.

Reading just wasn't my thing up until that point. I'd rather have basted myself in fantasy via a Zenith television and a Victoria Secrets catalogue than focus on a series of paragraph that would eventually and quite simply, wash right over me, like they'd never been read. Half a graph into any previous tale, my head would be gone, running straight into the arms of Cheryl Tiegs, dressed simply in an aqua blue string bikini, hugging on me and Mr. T after we slapped the shit out of some bad guys south of Texas, in some greasy town with a greasy name like, "Muddy."

But then, a mere twelve words in, I was hooked. And I mean really hooked on "The Outsiders" Again, like, I suppose, my obsession with rock and roll figures—outlaws like Elvis, Buddy and Waylon Jennings—the same characters they drew from in their songs no longer fit only within my eardrums. Now my mind raced from word to word instead of note to note, just dying to know what kind of bullshit these "outsiders" would be getting themselves into again.

Pony Boy, Soda Pop, Two-Bit, and my all-time favorite, Dallas, devoured me, soaked me into their world, walked all over me, made me envy for a slice of their disarray. The words they spoke, how they spoke them, when they spoke them cracked me in half, had me walking and talking just like them around my neighborhood, chucking attitude all the way. Faking it, as usual.

A Hinton book, to me, was always a relentless rush of passion and violence, paranoia and early love. Real love. Love from the prairies. Love from the tenement houses. Love looking up from beneath a Chevy stock engine. Mean love too. The kind that got you locked up. The kind that landed you on a gurney with six inches of steel cut into your belly. Jealousy, confusion, corrupted families. God, it was all so gorgeous to read.

My head swam at night and during the day when I would ride the throne, enjoying an evacuation, or tucked away in my bedroom, going from page to page, heart beating, not seeing the sun or feeling the air coming through my bedroom windows, the cries of my mother to "knock it off!" Not caring if I was missing a pick up game of touch football at a friends house. Not caring about anything but the words. Just the words.

The attitude inscribed in Hinton's text was enough for me to search out other writers of the same ilk. Thankfully, my brother, Mike, is a bright, bright lad, capable of commanding a room with a clean and precise dissertation on the stern outlook of death by John Updike, if he so wished. He can still can go for minutes on end about the worthlessness of delusionment without burping up a single "And, ah."

My brother surged with energy when he spoke about a book he liked, a writer, a topic. He confirmed for me that there is so much more to a book than just the story. There is the creator of the story, how they worked, failed, picked themselves up after a flurry of rejection letters. Or not. How the writer endured in life, marriage, work. He explained to me as we drank beer one glorious day in Key West what the song "Slip Sliding Away" by Paul Simon really means when you listen to the words. I promise, they will break you if you dare.

James Baldwin, Jim Harrison, Barry Hannah, these geniuses came into my life around the time I was pushing puddles of rain around a parking lot in Boston for $8 an hour. My mid 20s. Their words and characters presented themselves in a fashion I had no choice but to adopt. They just dangled so comfortably within my state of mind. Not my true existence, of course, but the other world I yearned to live in. Somewhere where the conversation didn't begin and end with the question, "So, do you have…?"

But that was years later, long before rejection stopped tasting so badly.

So, that was that. I read and I read and waited until my next chance to be something again presented itself. This whole "nothing" thing was starting to ring less and less true, though. I have to tell you that. It soon revealed itself clouded and shrouded in holes. The question my mother asked me countless times, "Who do you think you are?" started to flex into "Who do I want to be? Anyone I want." The more I read the more

I wished to change. Then return and change back again. Over and over, reworking the wool on my shoulders, the spin in my rod, the spit on my tongue. It was intense. There were just so many voices to hop up on, so many characters to identify with, to be disgusted by, to love and envy. Just the kind of people you want to take that magic carpet ride with. My options were endless.

Hinton first soaked me with her characters, the young toughs, men struggling to piece it all together in a world gone mad. Then it was "No One Here Gets Out Alive," a book about the rock band the Doors by Jerry Hopkins that hurried in a whole new layer of disenchantment into my life. Had me thinking about altering my own state of mind. Sounded very appealing, dipping into the ozone of my own madness, careening through the bile, the waste, the secrets never to be told.

"To Kill a Mockingbird" did nothing for me. I was too distracted, far too in love for the first time with a stunning Vietnamese/Chinese girl for that novel to penetrate my corroded heart. "A Separate Peace" made me loathe anything associated with prep schools for a good twenty years. I just "yawned myself to shit" as Bukowski would say, whenever I read anything centered around academia. It bored the shit out of me, too, Hank! "Animal Farm" was cool, somewhat. I mean, all the hogs and horses turning on each other ended up being a reality show years later. No pig was going to take on a pipe and some bike chain when it came slashing down on its hide during a back-alley rumble when the Greasers teamed up with the Socs for a nightly ass kicking on the hogs. And the horses? Just start throwing granny Smith green apples into the meadows. They'll go running. And Old Major? Kick his ass, too.

But in all these books, I did learn something. Something indeed: You can read to learn or you can read to live. I read to live. Somewhere within all those words was the voice I was looking for, the voice that would carry me out of this self-imposed prison of nothingness and put me where I was supposed to be in life. Not center stage, not backstage, but in the game, kicking up dust with everyone else. It would be a slow burn, this quest to be heard. But, I had time and the burn was working for me, not against me. Felt good to hurt for something.

And then I saw the bright lights of Plymouth shining off Interstate 93.

18. ROXBURY BUST

Most of the letters I received back from the dozen colleges throughout New England that I applied to before graduating from high school in 1988 read like this: "Find a trade, Jack."

I say most, but I really only mean one school out of twelve accepted my application. By the time letter six arrived at my home, I was pretty much just tearing and tossing without even opening the envelope. By then, I could recognize what a rejection letter looked like without even touching it. And it wasn't much to look at either. The envelope, sometimes beige, sometimes white or gray, always had a sterile look to it, just sitting there like some impotent geek on the kitchen counter, waiting to take away just a little bit more of my dignity as I slid a sheath under the tongue glued-envelope seal.

Indeed, it turned out to be a trade school that finally took me in. But nevertheless, a real college.

Wentworth Institute of Technology on Huntington Ave in Boston was no joke. Just up the road from Northeastern University, Wentworth has educated many men and women behind, I'm sure, a solid portion of the nation's highway infrastructure, suburban sprawl, new retail developments and big and small downtown renovation projects. Builders and engineers, heavy machinery operators, electricians, union bosses, welders, carpenters and so on. That's the kind of workers Wentworth produced. Real workers. And I was none of those things. Not even close.

A small school back in 1989, maybe 800 students, Wentworth was 15 stops (the very last stop) on the Orange Line out of Oak Grove Station in Melrose and into Roxbury. Winter nights could be tricky slogging your way off campus and through the housing projects with a T-Square strapped across your back, street lights already on, not knowing if the blood stories you read about on the train in the newspapers actually happened.

To be honest, I hardly even remember applying to Wentworth. After Keene State, Salem State, Westfield State and even Plymouth State College rejected me, I mean, my sky went black. I was floundering like a mofo. I needed to make a decision about what I was going to do with my life come the fall. I knew I wasn't ready to go to work 9-5. I had a hard enough time power edging someone's walkway when I worked for a landscaping company without blasting a stone into one of my coworkers eyes. I was a lazy fucker, too. I needed a nap once a day, still do. When I worked in Boston as a collections agent for a recording studio, I slept through lunch on a rooftop overlooking Mass. Ave when the weather was right. It was some of the best sleep I've ever gotten. When I worked in a steel yard as a supervisor on a union job out of Bow, New Hampshire, loading and unloading street plates, steel girders and water pipe, I slept shirtless on the bed of my pickup truck parked inside a mega sandpit surrounded by heavy equipment, like backhoe loaders, dozers and excavators. When I was driving around in a work van with a 300-gallon tank of frozen liquid oxygen in the back, logging 150 miles a day delivering to the homes of thousands of people struggling to breath throughout Greater Boston, I would regularly pull into a Walmart parking lot and catch a twenty-minute wink job. I'm a big proponent of napping, getting that extra charge, that final push you need to make it through the day.

My folks were getting pretty pissed off back then because it cost about $40 to apply to a college. So that added to their frustration with me and my existence. As adults, they knew where all this was going: Nowhere. Still, they paid and prayed, and when the first few letters came back addressed to some milk dud named "Jack" we all understood the administrations reasons for not welcoming me into their universities. I was reaching, thinking that such schools as the University of Massachusetts or the University of New Hampshire would accept my sorrowfully weak grades. Like I said, I was a straight-up C student with the rare B- and more than a few Ds tossed in the soup.

Like the story Leo Tolstoy told in his book, "A Confession," about the man who ran from a beast in the woods and dove into a well to save himself, only to realize that at the bottom of the well awaited a dragon that was ready to tear him apart. Death on both sides. So, halfway down the well the man reaches for a few small branches sticking out of the stone and saves himself, temporarily. Until he sees two mice come from

44

out of the stones and start eating away at the branches he held onto for dear life. He needed to decide whether he should climb back up to the top of the well and die at the hands of the beast. Or let go and fall into the dragon's vicious mouth. Contemplating his violent fate, the man hangs on and watches the mice chew at the limping limb and finally sees two leaves growing off the branches that are dripping with honey. Right then, the man make his decision: Fuck death. I'm going for the honey. So, he starts licking the leaves.

Wentworth was my honey. So, I tongued the shit out of it.

When I found out that four other friends from high school—Nosa, T-Bone, Lance and Bobby O—had all applied to Wentworth for various reasons and got in, I decided to follow suite. The other guys all came from blue-collar families that also worked hard in the construction business and promoted the idea of work and family as a singular notion. These young men had plans for a life in construction and demolition. Big pickup trucks, hefty paychecks, new homes with vaulted ceilings in the foyers, winters spent skiing in Maine and mixing up Margaritas to the exhausting sounds of Jimmy Buffett with the rest of the border rats from the Bay State getting buzzed up on "Big Dig" money. Not a bad way to live. And live they have, each to this day is still working and thriving in the construction business. Go Raiders! Yet, I yearned for none of those things.

But then I said, looking at my finite options, "What the hell? I can play the chameleon. Just call me 'Bob the Builder.'"

Problem was, I knew nothing and cared even less about building anything in my life. Never built a fort that held rain as a kid. Was disqualified from a Pinewood derby while in the Cub Scouts because the rig I threw together stalled out after a ten-foot push. And I hated dirt, mud, dust. I don't even like bending over much either, nevermind carrying around heavy sheets of drywall. Frankly, I don't know a carburetor from a generator, and I can barely take a door off a door hinge without referring to a Youtube tutorial. I say that jokingly, but it troubles me to this day how inept I am at doing "Manly Stuff."

Still, even if my fingers were too stubby and slick to grip a finish nail, I applied to Wentworth, was miraculously accepted and began classes for a degree in Building Construction in the fall of 1988. Slowly, I tried to morph into a future contractor. I bought some Red Wing work boots, a Carhartt jacket, started poorly growing a goatee and I stopped filing my nails at night. For a brief moment I would even pretend to engage in conversations about famed architect Frank Lloyd Wright's more heralded creations, and also lead the occasional heated discussions about how profound an effect the reconfiguring of the traffic scheme throughout Boston would enhance the driving experience instead of being trapped in the Callahan Tunnel, eating fumes for lunch.

But, almost immediately, instead of gaining interest in the masonry and design and civil engineering classes I was taking the first few weeks of the first semester, I found myself, instead, highly engaged in a curriculum required English class I attended a couple times a week. The class didn't feel much different than a high school English class—same number of students, same desks, same black-boards—but for some reason, I felt the urge to listen to the teacher this time around. It helped.

She had dark hair, she was Italian, I think, with dark circles under her eyes and on the motherly side of the dial. She wasn't tenured yet, but she was no rookie either. She didn't look beaten by the education system. She had energy and couth and she never tried to come off as being slick. She was a pro, engaging. And I bought into her completely from the "git-go" as they say. I can't name a story I read or an essay I wrote that stands out that she assigned, but the education I received came in the instructor who told the story, not just the story. She was the story, how she taught it, spoke of it, carried it beside her. Her name escapes me forever and a hardened sense of laziness keeps me from reaching her true identity, but this woman communicated in a way that finally gave me that reason to shut the fuck up and listen to something other than the raping of my own mind.

There was also a library on the small campus that was loaded with books and magazines, old newspapers and VHS cult movies like "Repo Man," "A Clockwork Orange," and "Eraserhead." I never watched these films in high school. I had no access to them. I didn't buy movies at a record store, I bought records. Video stores were just becoming a "thing" in the 1980s. Amazon? You kidding me? Today, one click and you get what you want. But then, you had to dig and scrape to find the good B-movies and dirty literature. I didn't have the resources, so I stuck to staring at scrambled porn on the Zenith.

Bricks and mortar, nope, that wasn't working for me. My fault too. The courses were just way over my head. My brain works in loops, and I need to do something 100 times before I'm ready to move onto the next thing.

I was getting quickly outpaced by the other students. The subject matter was beyond my intellect and interest. I liked the idea of being a "contractor," liked how it sounded and the image it gave off. But I was locked into a dreamer's delight, filled with art, culture, word and music. Nowhere in that dream did I see a jackhammer.

I started skipping all the construction classes and went only to my English class and some the other required courses. The rest of the time I was in the library, photocopying pages from old Esquire magazines that featured articles by and about Tennessee Williams, Arthur Miller and John Steinbeck. I was trying to read everything I could get my hands on that had anything to do with nothing I knew. The train I traveled on daily was built for reading, so I read, going back and forth from the burbs to the projects, projects to the burbs. I had all the time in the world to read. And if on that day I had watched a film, say, like "A Clockwork Orange," that would be enough to inspire me to read all I could about the author of the book the film was based on Anthony Burgess. I would need to know where Burgess came from and what drove him to delve into such violence and madness in his art? Was he himself a violent man? Did his mother try and break him too?

It wasn't as if I wasn't getting an education. It just wasn't the one my parents were paying for. Had they known how I was actually spending my days on their hard-earned dime digesting magazines, movies and pulp literature, they would have bludgeoned me on the spot. I really had no idea if all the hours I logged watching "On The Waterfront" would pay off for me down the road, but I was willing to roll the dice....their dice. Heathen.

After a week of sniffing piss on the Orange Line, me and the same guys I went to college with from my hometown would hit the road and visit our friends at "real" colleges. The colleges that looked like the ones on the pamphlets that arrived at my home with such promise during my senior year—then left with a fistfull of my pride. The same ones whose glossy covers were lined with trees and granite benches, faculty halls, science buildings, green grass and dormitories covered in vine.

Me and the boys had a solid college weekend touring schedule. Back then we'd pack the cars with pillows and chewing tobacco and take to the mighty hills of the Granite State or Western Massachusetts. We did some overnights at Colby Sawyer, at Keene, UNH, Dartmouth, even Harvard. And we found love in every town. Sometimes we had friends on campus.

Sometimes we just made friends. We were a chatty bunch and we all had fake IDs.

One week, an older buddy from Melrose, a guy named Mike O'Leary, invited us to come up one weekend to Plymouth State College. I knew nothing of the town or the college. It was a haul for my 1981 Toyota Corolla, about 100 miles from my hometown each way. I remember that. And she coughed the entire way up and back. But weekends were made for balling so we took 93 north and chugged our way to Plymouth. I was digging the black hills that fell to the west and the tree line to the east as we hooked turns through Tilton and New Hampton. The dark roads comforted me. I could feel my blood pressure drop for some reason. My breathing was less labored. My fingers stopped shaking, my teeth chattered less. There was just something about this area that cradled me as we cruised along and brought a calm to my senses and made me feel welcomed. The air that swam inside me as I traveled toward exit 25 had tripped the wires in my brain and forced me to relax, stay in the moment. Watch and listen. Again, just shut up.

I was unidentifiable on those roads. That's how I felt. I could be a trapper from New Bedford if I wanted to introduce myself as such. Maybe a webmaster from Boston working on some music sharing project. Then again, a pug-faced ninja fighter sounded ok too. I could be anything I wanted to be because my slate was clean in the Granite State. I knew nobody and nobody knew me. A stranger in a strange town. Something S.E. Hinton could really sink her teeth into. The runaway. "*A-run, run, run, run, runaway…*"

We hung out for a couple nights in Plymouth and I was pleasantly assaulted by the scene. Young women were EVERYWHERE! It was baffling. There was such an array of beauty that arose in my core that it imploded my mind to consider such an existence. We drank whisky and terrible beer and smoked weed out of tubes that stunk of old mouth and rotten water. I hadn't smoked much weed in the past, a few driveway hits now and again. But this time around, well, I made fast friends with this skunky, smelly dude named "Ed." Together, we met new faces, heard new voices styled by tongues born out of all corners of the northeast. Barely sleeping, instead opting to stay up till 4 a.m., piss drunk but lucid, wired on Ephedrine mostly, sitting outside with a handful of strangers on a broken picnic table adding more zest to each story told, I was calm, present, living within the moment. At home, it felt, for once.

Back in English class later that week, with the memories of the weekend at Plymouth State still stuck in my mind—the hills, the sticky dorms, the freedom to urinate out any backdoor, the open- aired conversations that blossomed between strangers, the erotic nature of a rare glance—those smells and sounds and sights were hammering away at me and I only wanted more of it.

That night, or soon after, I pulled one of my fathers old typewriter out of a closet, set it up on a plastic milkcrate in the basement of my home and got to work. I had one letter to draft and that was to the admissions board at Plymouth State College. I didn't even asked my parents about a transfer because there was a pretty good chance the college wouldn't take me in . . . again. Why annoy my folks even more, right? How much disappointment can two people take? I was but three months into my college career at Wentworth and I wanted out! They would have been so proud to hear the news! Such progress! I had fairly good grades up to that point in my required classes, but the actual engineering and math and science classes, well, that was a shit show.

Approaching the letter much in the same way I did the column I wrote in typing class years back, I wrote fearlessly, from the gut. I knew to keep it short, get some inspirational punch-up words in there when needed, do it clean, do it right. This letter needed to be more than a simple read. It needed to be heard! The board needed to understand that a bachelor's degree in English is what I really wanted at 19 years old. Not anything having to do with the blueprint of a condominium complex or the expansion of suburban sprawl. They needed to hear that although my grades were hideous in high school, a change had come over me. " *A new beginning has presented itself to me in the foothills of your town and I really need you to take a shot on me. Fate requires it.*" Maybe that was the formula I was missing all these years. Instead of spending all those arduous hours of my youth trying to figure out what I wanted to be, I should have simply decided right off what I didn't want to be. Don't like the outdoors? Then don't work outside. Hate people? Don't work in an office. Fear death? Become a mortician.

But mostly, I needed to put my heart into this letter and capture the attention of whoever opened it immediately. Sentence One. Go! Grip them by the throat. Stick a boot on their neck. So, I wrote the letter then tore it up. Wrote some more, tore more to shreds. I talked myself dry dictating my intentions. I bled over this proposal. I even called in the old big yellow pillow that bloodied my face while I watched Bruins games as a kid and punched at it repeatedly in frustration, sending echos of raw frustration banging off the basement panelling. The letter needed to be perfect! It needed to sell!

The letter and the application went out in the mail sometime before winter, and by the start of my last semester at Wentworth, I received a letter addressed to "Robert" not "Jack" from Plymouth State College, welcoming me into the fold. I was elated. Finally, I felt inside, like my apprenticeship from being a nothing to something had ended. This was a turning point. One where there was nobody to blame but myself if the experience ended up in the shitbox. And although I didn't know it yet, soon I would find my calling, my own quest to be heard laid out right before me in the hills of Plymouth. It was all right there—my audience, the stories, the vices and voices that carried out those stories, all of it, right there, just ripe for the picking.

It was my time to roar.

19. A FAN'S NOTE

Six months into Plymouth State College and I had already got myself kicked out of Hall Dormitory for racking up too many misconduct referrals. Night One, I mean, really, the very first night I spent on campus, the very same night I met the same group of friends that I'm proud to say I still see regularly today, we all snuck beer into the dorm and drank bountiful amounts of Milwaukee's Best and carried on about who we were and where we came from. Strike One! Night One! We were written up by the residential director for drinking in our rooms. Four more minor offenses (booze and noise violations) later and I would be cast out into the streets of Plymouth, on my own to find comfort and shelter.

Still, ecstatic with our newfound freedom to twist tales and take on any persona we wished, we shouted like banshees that night, beating our bare chests, layering our lores with mystique, not knowing from that day forward we would all be friends forever, sharing in the good, the bad and the ugliest of moments life has to offer—like marriage, divorce, the birth of children, the loss of children, federal indictments, debt, curfews, illnesses, and, of course, countless evenings filled with wild abandonment teetering on lunacy.

I was introduced to guys named Snake and Sweet Lou, Pat The Rat, Waldo, Brady, Johnny Boy, Money, Freddy, Big Joe and Jeffro. They came from towns I never heard of, like Dover and New Boston, Seekonk, Goffstown and Windham. There was also this 225-pound Iranian guy on our floor named Kambez who came from Cambridge and continually ran up and down the halls slamming back beers, bragging about the enormous thatch of pubic hair he carried between his thighs, shouting. "Yeah, man! I got big bush! Kambez got big bush!"

I mentioned earlier on that I didn't do very well in the friend depart ment growing up. I was a terrified prick loaded with a million insecurities. I couldn't shake myself, my fears, my resistance to putting myself out there. Sackless to the core. Today, I see my 16-year-old daughter, Danielle, play bassoon in the school jazz orchestra after training since grade school, and I am crippled with envy. Making it about myself, somehow always, I watch the team of musicians on stage perfectly execute "Band of Brothers" to the timing of the conductor's stick and jealousy races through my loins. It's inspiring, mind boggling, pride-producing stuff that makes your skin turn to chicken and your eyes well up. But it's also difficult to witness because within all that beauty I flashback to my days of nothingness when I could have been right there on stage, turning screws with all the other artists—all the other "geeks"—but instead I sulked and snickered, acted the fool and wasted time. Stupid.

That's why I didn't spare a minute that first night at Plymouth State trying to immerse myself into the lives of these young men. I wasn't taking any chances this time around. I needed them more than they needed me. They just didn't know it. And instead of hiding behind the same cloak of insecurity I wore in the past, I tore the lid off the top and said, "Fuck it!" Going forward, I would approach friendship as if it means something, as if my life depended on it. And it did. I had failed so many times in the past as a friend that I feared karma was catching up to me. No more. Never again. I would treat friendship with respect, listen to everything it had to say, every sweet nugget it had to offer.

Years back, I would bully my way into someone's life, grinding them into submission in order for them to call me a friend. A cheap trick, but I was desperate then. But not this time around. Not this night in Plymouth. I was wide open and more than willing to share the rest of my life with these guys—if they would have me. I didn't know their last names until weeks later, calling them instead by nicknames like "Triple Nipple," "Wall Eyed Bass," and "Meat Man." Still, I felt reborn beside them. I could carry myself as if "nothing" ever happened, like my past had been erased. I was working with a new canvas and all I wanted was some purity within my intentions. And a fair share of madness.

Academically, I was on the "2.0 and Go" plan. Once again, just like at Wentworth, I was doing the bare minimum in my required courses— geography, science and math classes—because my focus was on literature as I worked toward a liberal arts degree. I just loathed all the other classes that had nothing to do with character growth and climax. I walked into a trigonometry class my freshman year, then walked out, never to return.

"F." But my literature classes, well, that was like getting cracked with a bullwhip on the ass and liking it as you beg for more lashings. ("Turn me purple, Butch!")

Accomplished scholars, novelists and poets instructed me, guided me, tested me, hated me and befriended me. They were like my Italian English professor at Wentworth but on the needle and bean. Dr. Robert Garlitz introduced me to the poets William Blake and Robert Lowell. Astounded by the images these men created with their works, I loved struggling to understand their message. Their sentence structures were a huge blur of beauty to me. What did Blake mean when he wrote, "Troubled wilderd and forlorn, Dark benighted travel-worn" in "A Dream?" No clue, but it sounded so good, so rich with life, so poetic. I chugged down on those words and let them spill upon my chest.

And the spin Dr. Garlitz put on explaining the text was equally jarring. Thin built with glasses, a bald head, sharp-nose and a slow way of walking and talking, this man Garlitz appeared to me, at the time, to be completely mad. Absolutely bat-shit crazy. A true original, a relentless game player, a real mind fucker when he chose to be. And, I mean that in the most complimentary way. Often, I felt like I was receiving my lessons from the bowels of an opium den when Garlitz would lecture on, say, Jack Kerouac's "The Dharma Bums." His method of teaching was that relaxed, that intoxicating, that interpretive. Garlitz didn't tell you what the poet meant for you to read, he allowed you to digest it anyway you pleased. Allowing a poem to land on you is one thing. Asking it to bath in your skin and thoughts for hours after reading it, well, that's what Garlitz taught me to go in search for. So I did.

Mr. Gerald Zinfon was another influential professor of mine who didn't bother to dabble in sugary lectures. With his hard and round wine-loving belly pressed out to the class and his growling sense of demeanor, Zinfon showed us that if you had a conscience and a brain, you could write poetry. Poorly, of course, at first. But every man and woman has at least one great poem in them. That's what I learned from Zinfon, that if you can manage to find your own voice, you've won half the battle. As elusive as that voice can be, once discovered, the literary game is yours to enter. Batter up!

The best poem I ever wrote (one of maybe a half dozen) came from an assignment Zinfon dished out to the class one day. "Go home and write a poem." I can hear him say as he turns away from the class. "You can leave now."

On his command, and not just because Mr. Zinfon was a former Marine who served in the Korean conflict, and not just because Zinfon was an incredible poet himself, I rushed back to my apartment and wrote "The Wish" and it went like this: *In the warmth of the sheets of my own bed, I wish to lie like a fetus until I'm dead.* That's it. That's the best poem I ever wrote. Damn thing was all about being hungover, face in the bucket, wasting away in my own stink. Likely, nine out of ten "real" poets would shrug both shoulders and muffle under their breath, "It's OK." And they would be right. It is just OK. But it was my best OK, and it felt pretty damn good, not just to write it, but to read it over and over again to myself, melding my creation and putting some shine on the composition.

Zinfon approved of the poem and it ended up in the PSC Literary Review of Fiction and Poetry. Not since typing class had I felt so vindicated. Not really knowing what I was being acquitted of, I still felt like I was moving closer towards something when I learned that my poem would be one of twenty seven selected works accepted into the periodical. This was big to me. Recognizing its limited relevance in the battle-scarred World of Words, I considered this honor to be just one of many stepping stones I would need to cross in order to be heard. I said to myself, "This is my hustle, this is my thing. Let's do this."

Then, all hell broke loose when I was assigned a novel called "A Fan's Notes" by Frederick Exley. I was introduced to this writer by another writer named Joseph Monninger, who happens to be one of the three horsemen in this trilogy of influence that came upon me in the hills of Plymouth.

The handsome rascal, fresh off the success of his highly acclaimed novel, The Viper Tree, about a Nazi soldier who flees Europe for West Africa where his life gets tornado flipped, Monninger was that English professor I always figured on getting when I would finger through those fancy ivy-covered college pamphlets that teased me throughout my senior year of high school. He was bearded, broad shouldered with movie star looks and he was captivating. A former football star from New Jersey, Monninger was practical, approachable, forward thinking, even corny at times, an avid outdoorsman who wore his fishing vest downtown covered in lures and flies once while we shared a beer at one of the pubs.

A writer's writer, deadly serious about the craft, Monninger was a gift that almost whispered when he spoke, suggesting writers and stories and books to me that he knew I needed to read in order to embark on this personal "quest" of mine. Joe seemed to recognize the quest, relating to its hunger, patterns and disappointments. And the look in my eyes.

One day in class, Monninger started handing out "A Fan's Notes" for the students to read. I was figuring on getting more Steinbeck, more Papa Hemingway, more of those languishing wartime tales of bravado and portraits of the unfathomable cruelty taking place down South. So, I was happy to see when I had received my copy of "A Fan's Notes" that we had left the sparkling 20s and the blight atomic world of the 40s and made our way into a more modern age.

I flipped over to the back cover of the book and saw right away that this writer named Exley never spent a day in West Egg as I eyed his profile and brief bio. I liked this guys beard, his gray headed comb-over, how he touched a match to his cigarette, almost snickering in the black and white photo. He looked weathered in his dark wide collared golf shirt. I like weathered looking writers. He looked like a sad guy, and I'm a closeted sad guy. So, I liked that. He didn't live in Spain or London, Ireland or Los Angeles. He lived in upstate New York, near Ontario in a place called Watertown.

Before Monninger had the chance to begin his introduction of the book to the class, I had already read the first page and was flipping over to page 2. The words: *"On Sunday, the eleventh of November, 196—, while sitting at the bar of the New Parrot Restaurant in my hometown, Watertown, New York, awaiting the telecast of the New York Giants Dallas Cowboys football game, I had what, at the time, I took to be a heart attack."* squeezed the air out of me, bolting my feet to the floor. Now, to some, those words might not strike you with the eloquence of Dickens or the ferocity of Dostoevsky. But to me, those words said it all, showed me that a person is allowed to write with an alarming amount of brutal honesty and vulnerability, and when they do, with good intentions, with a quiet flair, it will seize the reader, bring them to their knees, help them to recognize something within themselves. It happens.

I attached myself to the the image of that man sitting in a bar, likely the first patron of the day, ordering a cold beer before noon, half a pack of smokes deep, jittering on the insides like a teen awaiting a snow day announcement because his beloved New York Giants were going to play football and he was going to watch it on the television . . . all day long!

I know that sense of euphoria . . . and defeat. I chase it twice a week, then choke on the remains of that fleeting joy twice more. The smell of that bar, the touch of something sweet or sour on your lips at an unfamiliar hour, readying yourself in the cave you chose to inhabit, longing for a glimpse of promise, not sunshine, talking shit with other shit talkers. Just watching the games.

The Gardens of Versailles in France had nothing on Exley's haunt, the New Parrot.

So, I read and I read and I couldn't stop reading this book. I both loved and was disgusted with the main character, "Ex." He was lazy, half-baked in the head, a monumental bullshitter and certainly brilliant in some slothish manner but always feeding off someone elses tit. Neither valent or terribly masculine, Ex was, well, he was like a lot of people I knew. Starting with myself. But the world had beat his ass good and red. He knew it. The world knew it. So be it.

And the writer of those words, Frederick Exley, wrote heroically, sentence after sentence in this "fictional memoir." He left the reader with something profound to chew on every page, really, and, frankly, just kept things moving. Once you think Ex has torpedoed his life for the final time, he ends up in a nuthouse receiving electroshock treatment, or quitting on AA or a marriage or recounting his raging adulation for New York Giant's star running-back, Frank Gifford, while pining for sex with his personal minx, Bunny. I loved this guy.

The impression the book left on me was simple: that's how I wanted to write. Open throated, tossing literary haymakers into the crowd, seeing what lands with a bang or limps sadly off the page, forgotten forever. If Exley chose to nail himself to the cross for the sake of art, well, then, I would too. You have to bleed for your art. There is no in-between. Or at least try, right? Why not? Nothingness, I learned through Ex, through Monninger and Zinfon, Dr. Garlitz and my steel circle of friends, wasn't something to try and defeat any longer. Its days were numbered. But not before I revealed the welts, the risks, the fears and lies that borders my brain, putting nothingness on blast.

Only problem was: I had no place to blast, no place to publish my confessions.

20. SPANKIN' IT

After a brief conversation with a new friend I had made in yet another literature class during my sophomore year at Plymouth State, I soon realized that the most I was going to get out of this class was, well, just about everything I ever wanted. Maybe more than I wanted.

At least that's how it turned out.

The class was lead by a past middle-aged professor who appeared to be running on fumes, working out of a yellow ledger book, decades old. Between being bored to shit by the man's motionless delivery and perpetual lack of oomph, myself and this new friend of mine, Dave Cummings, would jaw back and forth before, during and after class about a vast array of things, like sex and sex and pretty much more sex.

Dave, a man with a wiry, rope muscle build, a high hairline, hopped up on a pink cloud of sobriety, hailing from the mean streets of Newport, had already been thrown out of four colleges before he found his way to Plymouth State. Hard to imagine, at first, for me, this gentleman, this quick-thinking, well-informed, highly energetic and productive guy, just a couple years older than me, had managed to get tossed off four campuses. That's some impressive numbers. In order to pull off such a feat, you would have to have one hell of a story to tell. So I listened. Buried under all that laughter, that fire wit, somewhere between, as Mr. Dylan would say, "Love and Theft" Dave was, and still is, one of my biggest mentors.

Then again, I always wondered if Dave was removed from all those campuses for bearing a tattoo of the "Pink Panther" on his left shoulder. I never asked. I should ask. Seems like a credible reason for an expulsion.

Dave not only told some of the most hilariously vile stories with the flair of a true artist, but he was also the editor-in-chief of the college newspaper, *The Clock*. He ran the small paper and worked the sports pages with the professionalism of any *New York Times* sports writer or editor. He took great pride in a solid, clean layout. I would often read Dave's column or write ups on the Celtics or any sports team at school and walk away informed, entertained and influenced in some way. He wrote better than anyone I had ever met. And I hadn't met any really good writers up to that point. I had read many good writers. I just didn't know any of them. Other than Dave.

One day, just before class began, Dave asks me if I wanted to write for *The Clock*. I don't remember hesitating saying yes, not for a moment. I was honored to be asked. But then, and pretty quickly, I started to get anxious about what I agreed to do. I'm great at saying "Yes" to things. But, I'm also abnormally lazy. This started to sound like real work. Dave told me he would assign me a story or two, easy stuff.

"Oh, Jesus," I remember thinking. "Tell me I won't have to write about what hot lunches are being served in the cafeteria this week." Seeing that Dave and I had quickly developed a bond that centered around the sadness in both our father's eyes, our vices to overcome and lust for life, I felt very comfortable saying to Dave, *"Tell me I won't have to write about what hot lunches are being served in the cafeteria this week."*

It wasn't that I was above mucking it out in the trade, learning the ropes, licking the curb at the bottom to start. I just knew I would totally suck at writing like that. That kind of writing requires discipline. It requires great skill for formatting and word usage. There was nothing loose about reporting. I needed to be loose. And, I didn't want to let Dave down.

The dilemma was one I would wrestle with for the better half of a decade, figuring out what I couldn't do first, then turning around and doing something else. For instance, years after graduating from college, when I was offered a job with a small Boston newspaper called the "Boston Metro," where I would share in covering the homestands of the Boston Red Sox during the 2002 season. I got to file short boxscore stories about the hometown team for an entire summer and watch Derek Lowe pitch a no-hitter for the Sox from the media room directly above home plate at Fenway Park. I was in the locker rooms, the press conferences, standing around the dugout during batting practice. A hack like me gets a job like that once in a lifetime. It was a dream gig, if you were really—and I mean "really"—into sports. You had to live and breathe it. Whether you could catch a football or not, if you were in the trade of sports writing, you had to be all in. It's a time-consuming, pressure-cooking profession with layers of details to cover that sometimes takes a magician to make work.

Which, in the end, as a beat writer, I never had in me.

But the job did have its perks. Late one afternoon, I walked into a Red Sox game through the media gate with none other than Mike Barnicle, the beloved then tarred and feathered *Boston Globe* city columnist who got caught making stories up and was quickly ostracized, banished to the Hall of Shame. I had read Barnicle's columns growing up, my father did too, as did my brother and his friends, their aunts and grandparents and every crooked politician skulking their way around the State House, biting into my take home pay. Everyone read Barnicle. He was a legend from the "old school" of newspaper writing, I guess, where everyone he knew was always Jimmy or Timmy or Tommy or Terry. That kind of tired bullshit. Once a God in the city of Boston. Now, not so much.

I thought that was pretty cool, like I had somehow made it, if not inside the circle, then pacing around the backside, working my way in slowly.

All the heavy hitters from the New England sports writing world hung around the media room on game day—Dan Shaughnessy, Gordon Edes, Peter Gammons, Steve Buckley, Jackie MacMullen and a young Tony Massarotti, who, then, I think, was writing sports for the *Boston Herald*. The squealing pitch of Massarotti's voice could be heard from the back row of the bleacher seats where the smaller newspapers worked with such clarity that his screech would stop you in your tracks from finishing a sentence. Maz.

The other writer that I split the season with was the great Alex Speiers, today the incredible sports writer for the *Boston Globe*. Alex quickly rose up the ranks with his clean and devastatingly well researched pieces. He could dissect the sequences of a designated hitter and middle reliever over 800 words and leave you jonesing for more facts and figures. Soon, Alex would be a regular on all the local Boston sports shows, offering direct insights on the Celtics, Sox, Bruins and Patriots. I often watch Alex dish on Tom Brady or Big Papi and think, "Man, if I could have only written even somewhat like Alex I could be grinding it out with that "ass hat" Mike Felger on television, trying not to let him get over on me.

But, alas, it never would be. I was horrendous at filing a story on time. I couldn't keep track of the innings, who was pitching, who just hit one up the gap or what the fuck the score was. Everything went so fast. The other writers tore into their pieces, had them written in their heads before the end of the game whether the team won or lost. It seemed like they all knew just where to put every word, fill out every inch of the limited space allotted by their editors. Me? I was in the back row with a line of sweat running down the crack of my ass, trying to remember who pitched in the game and whether the boys took home the win.

I had a handful of great moments covering the Red Sox that summer, like interviewing the Hall of Famer and stolen base phenom, Rickey Henderson, who, when he spoke caused me to stand mesmerized by the number of times he referred to himself as "Rickey" as if he was talking about another player on the team. I kept turning my head around, thinking there was some other player named Rickey behind me. Branch Rickey? There wasn't. It was just "Rickey being Rickey" before Manny was Manny.

That was the fun part of the job . . . sometimes.

Other times, when you would have to bow down and kiss the ring of some 22-year-old kid who sat wrapped up in a towel of ice and happened to be gifted in ways that allowed him to pick and choose who he decided to speak to, well, at times (many times) that was difficult for my ego to take. Grabbing a quote or two was pretty easy. But getting spit in the eye and ignored wasn't something I was interested in building up a tolerance for. So, and with good reason, (I sucked at it), I bowed out of that style of writing and sought a different avenue to pursue. I got a taste of the good life, a behind-the-scenes look at the the Big Time world of sports. Yet, at the end of the day, I wasn't doing any service to this brand of writing, nor was I enjoying it, so I went back to being strictly a Red Sox fan.

Moving on . . .

"You can write about anything you want," Dave told me when I explained my hesitations in writing for the school newspaper. " You can even have your own column."

My own "column?" Now you're talking, Davey Boy!

We were speaking the same language, Dave and me, knowing that if I could translate in 700 words some of the very conversations we were having on a regular basis about the madness, the psychotic and lonely nature of our very dreams, it might be funny for a bit to write about them. I had no experience in this, not since typing class in junior high school, but I had read "Fear and Loathing in Las Vegas" by Hunter S. Thompson and "A Fan's Notes" by Exley. The poetry of Charles Bukowski was in my bones, their voices were in my head.

I knew where all this was going, so I ran with it.

But the column would need a catchy title, we both agreed. Something that pops and fires hot steam fresh out of the gate. Similar to the twenty minute clock I had to beat in Mrs. Mahoney's typing class, my deadline to obtain readers was now, I believed, set at a month or two. Six columns, no more. After that, I as was either in or out. Dave would see to that.

"We should call it "Whacking It" because all you do is whack it." Dave suggested as we fingered through an book of clip art, hoping to match the title up with a cool image.

"Interesting, interesting." I said, pondering the tone of the title, not disagreeing with the premise.

Immediately, I saw a cartoon of a bald guy who looked just like a mini "Mr. Clean." He had his fist cocked, his shirt sleeves rolled up over his meaty forearms, spit flying off his brow, ready to bust someone's lip. I loved it.

"Him!" I said, pointing to the picture. "Let's use that picture. And let's call the column, "Spankin' It.""

Done. We had the title. We had the image, and we even drew in the number "33" to look like a tattoo on Mr. Clean's shoulder, obviously to honor the greatest basketball player of all time, Larry Bird. Now, all I had to do was reach into my imagination and write like a crazy man. I knew what the readers wanted because I was in and out of every keg party both on and off campus, talking to legions of pent-up horn balls sucking back Keystone Lights, expounding on their wicked ways. I had made friends with jocks, shady dudes, hillbillies, poets and self-loathing prophets. Their interests seemed to rest in the grotesque misbehavior of one another, the shock of learning that they weren't alone in their sexual tendencies.

So, I figured, if we're all doing it, let's talk about it.

I did indeed write about sex, sometimes in a manner that shames me today when I look back on what I wrote—how poorly I wrote—twenty-five years later. Henry Miller I was not. I rambled a lot, took the long way home to get to a point. I wrote as I spoke, choppy and harsh. I wrote how I felt, dysfunctional and angry. And some of what I wrote embarrasses me as I sit alone in a cold basement, reading my old Spankin It columns.

By today's standards "Spankin' It" was pretty passive. It would have fit right in with some of today's more titillating writings on sites like "Barstool Sports." I talked about T&A, spoke poorly of both sexes, contradicted myself, inflamed the truth, boasted about nothing. It was all in fun.

In one column I admitted to being a bit of a troll at the college cafeteria, where, I think, I held a meal plan for nearly four years. It was an idyllic setting for watching women. I would gather my grub with my chums and we would find a spot to perch and gawk at these beauties filing past us, hot trays in hand, looking sensational. At times, there were a few of these wonders who really played up their cat walk through the cafeteria, knowing all eyes were on them. So, I wrote about a couple standouts, trying to disguise their identities with cute monikers, then, utterly failing in the end.

"... I have been forced this year to watch, one in particular, who I am nicknaming "Fashion Bug" and her friend "Sidekick," who roam the caf with their perfectly teased hair and tight miniskirts. I can hardly believe that I am complaining about this, but it's really annoying ... In their minds, they are the closest thing to a Playboy centerfold. Well listen up ladies, I haven't missed an issue in the last seven years, and you don't have a prayer..."

A bit boorish, yes. I could have—should have—omitted "Playboy," but by college standards, this was run-of-the-mill banter. Well, Fashion Bug and Sidekick saw things differently, tag teaming me one night after the column ran at a beer bash—and not in the cool way. They sought me out in the crowd, came charging right for me, pushing and cussing, chewing and spitting at me for dissing them as I did. How dare thy! They didn't seem to mind the press, it was the portrayal that got them steaming. I pretending not to care, just trying to get away from them, avoiding my responsibilities, running away from my words, my actions. But I hated that it happened. Can't stand when someone's mad at me. Worst feeling ever.

At the weight room one day in the athletic field house, I was standing at one of the leg racks avoiding doing squats. Two players from the football team were at the rack next to mine, having a heated conversation. One of the players, a hulk of a man with a thick head and neck and barn width shoulders, was making a gesture like he was going to break someone's neck. A bird? An opposing quarterback? Settling in under the bar, I tried to overhear who these two Mack trucks were talking about.

This nugget could be of good use in my next column, I thought, as I was now fully invested in my weekly tirades. Then I heard all I needed to hear.

"If I ever see that fuckin' kid, I'm going to kick the shit out of him. Who is this asshole?"

Ah, that would be me, sir.

As they both railed on about this "asshole," I remembered that I had recently written a column called *"Weight Room, Eye Boogers and MTV"* and made mention that the weight room hours could be more evenly tailored to fit equally amongst the student body and the student athletes. Heavy stuff.

"With all due respect to the Panthers, do we really need special hours for the team to workout? You guys and the girls are great, but we're not exactly the Miami Hurricanes or the Fighting Irish, now, are we?"

Needless to say, by demeaning the students and their athletic prowess, my catty comments—which were strictly motivated by envy—I rankled a few hearty Panthers, placing myself on the campus "Most Wanted" list. Never did I receive that beating by the boys, but they did find out who I was, and one of the players—surely an offensive lineman—whenever he would see me would stink-eye me to death, seething with fury, wishing he could cave my face in.

Like a skit, though, I just tried to get a rise out of the campus and see just how far I could go with this fleeting moment. This was my chance to act on my dreams, to walk the walk and talk it too. And, as my editor and dear friend Dave once said, "Don't be a dreamer that accomplishes shit."

There was a rawness in my quest to be heard and I was communicating the only way I knew how, writing the only way I cared to write, mimicking much of the time my own literary heroes. Looking back on the old pieces, I have to only read a few sentences before I am pretty disappointed with my own mind. It was me, all me, that's for sure. My thoughts, my actions, my ego that burned to be heard. At times, writing like I was desperate for attention, other times terrified to see in print what I had written nights earlier—likely high on grass—about my personal life, the home I was raised in, my grooming techniques and the people that shaped my existence, I felt morally corrupt, broken in parts.

My wife of eighteen years, Flower, whom I began dating when I started writing for the newspaper back in 1992, had made me a scrapbook of all my pieces and the piercing letters to the editor by some of the towns-people and a good many of the students wrote to the paper, demanding me removed from the masthead.

The Vice President of Student Affairs at the college, Mr. Richard Hage, had me in for a meeting soon after the first few columns appeared in *The Clock*. He was very nice, very fatherly, a true gentleman, and he explained to me that what I write today might just haunt me down the road. He was right. A few years later, when I was working as an teacher's aide in the special education department at Plymouth Regional High School in Plymouth NH, the head of the school board caught wind that I was work-ing at the school and promptly let me go. He knew the column, had read it and was repulsed by it. "Oh, please." I thought. "You and your virgin ears. I'm gone." I cared but I didn't. I fought the termination and lost. Then I just kept writing.

There was another time when a professor in the English department asked me to sit down with him at his office one day so he could scold me on what I wrote, how I wrote, and, basically, how ignorant a person I was. I didn't know this man, never had him as a professor. But I looked at him, he looked at me, and I could tell right off that he was not Dr. Garlitz, Mr. Zinfon or Joe Monninger. And, as I studied his face, red with hatred, I realized that what I had accomplished in such a short time gaining read-ers, well, for some reason, that really bothered him. At least that's the vibe I was picking up. And that was the hole in his argument, so I took a hard pass on his whining and moved on.

News of the column didn't just stick to the mean streets of Plymouth. An editor of another small paper in Lincoln, about 30 miles up the road, decided to decry my works by publishing portions of my pieces in *The Ideal's Free Local Paper*. Bad move. The local folks enjoyed getting their weekly fix of clean town chatter—the listings, coupons and police logs. Local stuff, like yard sales and maple gatherings over hot cider. The people of Lincoln did not take kindly to the editor, Joy L. Greenwood's, decision to reprint portions of my articles. What they read shocked most people and the paper immediately lost one of its largest advertisers. Greenwood told *The Clock* in an interview back in 92' that soon after her editorial ran, "Business took a brutal beating."

That was unfortunate.

Often, when the column came out, I both loved the attention and hated it. I wanted it, but I didn't. It was my dirty fix to play the Pusher Man, the shit stirrer, the wild man on campus who wrote the unspeakable. Much of what I wrote about was a free therapy session with myself where I assumed everyone else was suffering through the same angst of being a young adult as I was. I wrote about self love, yes, but I also touched on being rejected in love, loneliness, struggling to navigate your way through this maze called life, drunk and horny most days. It was relatable, it was in your face, at times irresponsible, and very well read.

In a town like Plymouth it's easy to get noticed, what with a population of only about five thousand people. Some of the townies were locked right into the college scene and read *The Clock* regularly too. They hated how I depicted their town and some of them hated me. Some of the cops didn't think too kindly of me either. That became problematic. I was arrested four times. Unlike my days back in the dorms where I was being written up for committing minor offenses, my actions became criminal. I was arrested for obstruction of justice, disturbing the peace, DWI, simple assault. This was the direct result of me buying into my own bullshit, lathering myself up like I was some Gonzo character, once again acting the fool. Ridiculous.

Then it was over, my brief brush with notoriety. The column, which ran for a couple years, started lifting its skirt to any cheap john, going from a belly-busting laugh to a mere chuckle over the course of two years. I was out of gas. My act dried up. Shit got old. It happens.

But I did what I came to do, and that was to be heard. My quest was very much alive. And what I learned in writing Spankin' It was that by putting myself out there, acting on my intuition, my instincts and by challenging others in conversation and working at my craft, that was something I planned to continue doing. It was also my last hoorah as far as bash writing, where I would single out people or customs and rip them to pieces. Who was I to tear anyone to shreds? If anyone was going to be hacked on in my future works, it would be me first.

Also, I was in no rush to be heard again anytime soon because I simply wasn't ready for the next phase of this quest. I would need to, as the great Southern writer Harry Crews said, "Put my ass in the seat" and get to work if I wanted to call myself a writer, which I have never done. All these ideas in my head weren't going anywhere. The ecstasy saw to that. It was my voice that needed to be developed. No longer would a flacid imitation of Hunter Thompson and Frederick Exley do justice. That scam had been run. And although the toxicity of their words would always influence my works, to be a cheap duplication would to be a failure. That I knew.

Now what?

21. TROUBLE IN NOVA SCOTIA

It was sometime in late August, the Summer of 2000, when we drove off that boat ramp into Yarmouth, Nova Scotia, ready to begin our lives together, legally, as a committed couple.

It should have been the time of our lives.

After a stellar ceremony on Cape Cod where friends and family drank themselves swollen, my new bride, Flower, planned our honeymoon around the seacoast of Nova Scotia. Our first stop would be to a romantic fishing town named Digby, located along the Bay of Fundy, about a two-hour drive from Yarmouth.

We were anxious to see if our decision to marry after ten relatively painless years of dating would enlighten the relationship. I had my doubts. Worse than that, I was certain that marriage was the cruelest sacrament of them all, a fairytale saddled with distance, resistance and resentment.

Still, I bought into marrying Flower for a million right reasons. Sure, she was (and still is) humble, funny, deliciously brown skinned and sincere. The Best of the Best. Quite impossible for me to have done any better.

Yet, long before the full spectrum of Flower's beauty presented itself to me; she teased me one afternoon with a gesture of loyalty I'd not soon forget. The gesture read: I'd walk on knives for you.

Not long after we started "dating," or whatever it is two people do in that mess known as college, I found myself in a jam with the local authorities, the result of one of those Late Night Overreactions.

It's a common fools story, so let's move on.

But the town law was on their way to visit me a couple days after the "overreaction." I'd been sitting in my apartment in front of the television set for the last four hours, waiting to a see any Springsteen video MTV had in the rotation.

It was 1991.

While I tried piecing together a ham and cheese sandwich out of a half slice of pickle and something that looked like mayonnaise, one of my roommates came humming up the stairs and tells me a cop just pulled up in front of the apartment.

So long sandwich. Out the back door I went, racing towards Flower.

I get to her place and I'm panicked beyond. Yes, beyond.

I'm shouting before she even answers the door of her student condo, "Where'd you say you were from?! Where? Where? Where?"

"Wha? What?" she's saying at the door.

"Where'd you grow up?! Where you from?"

"Upstate New York. Rochester. Why?"

"Let's go to Rochester."

All Flower said was, "Okay. Let's go."

And off we went. Just like that. No questions asked. No judgment. No schooling or scolding. Never had I felt such a full-sense of devotion before in my life. Or since.

So, one this first day of our marriage, she had agreed to take my heart and all my baggage to boot as we boarded the *Scotia Prince*. And the gods of fate would begin to test not only our faith, but both our nuts, and see just how strong we'd stand together.

As my faded out Honda Accord rolled down the boat plank, Flower greeted the crisp, sunny morning with fervor. Dressed in beige Capri pants, flat-soled shoes and an unforgivably revealing V-neck orange summer top. She looked spectacular, fresh and anointed.

With my brides leg swung over my lap, a border inspector approached our car and asked our reasons for coming to Canada. Flower said to the official, cute like: "We're on our honeymoon! We can't wait!" Then she plunged her French tipped left hand out the driver's side window, proving it proudly.

"That's great," the inspector replied, probably saying to himself, "Sweet knock off, femme."

Then he pointing towards a few empty parking spaces and said, "Now, head over there, please."

I dropped my sunglasses onto the bridge of my nose as the man with the badge pointed "over there." Over there wasn't where any of the other cars were heading. A caravan of sport cars and utility vehicles were closing in on downtown Yarmouth. We were heading in the opposite direction, towards a small brick building with sharp corners and tight parking spaces out front.

As I steered slowly towards two uniformed officers, I pushed Flower's legs off my lap, knowing nothing good was to come of this. "The hell's going on here, Flower?" I said to my new wife.

Sitting there all orange and committed while I suffered with rot on my tongue, Flower said, "Relax, honey," her voice shrinking unnaturally. "This is probably just what they do." Yeah, right.

We had a problem.

The night prior to docking in Yarmouth, I enjoyed a fatty on the deck of the Scotia Prince, which I had rolled the day before in Portland, Maine as we waited in line with the other vehicles to board the cruise liner. One tiny knot of grass, that's all. Barely a joint. More like a celebratory whack.

Over the night water, with the moon, the wind, the slap, slap, slap of the sea, I felt reborn, slightly, as I took that joint right down to the nub, then brought the roach back to my cabin and tucked it into a gym bag.

Standard stuff, no?

The inspector asked us to step out of the car. My hands swelled and lips cracked. Flower remained composed as the inspector rummaged through the ashtray and glove compartment, performing a standard inspection. We watched from a few feet away while Flower assured me everything would be fine.

We were anything but fine.

Stepping out of the car, the inspector asked me, "Do you have any marijuana on you, sir?"

"No." I said quickly. "Course not."

"I found seeds and stems on the driver's seat," he said. "Park the car. You're both being detained."

Right there I cursed the sacrament of marriage, kicked it right in the face. I knew it: Marriage was a curse!

Flower looked terrible. Her glow was gone, along with the pride she so briefly felt for her new husband. Sitting in a small office, I planned our defense after telling the inspector there was nothing left to find, offering this: "Pot gives me cankers. Many people drive this car. Please, it's our honeymoon."

We were both stripped-searched. My Flower went first with two female guards. I sat silently in a room with a male inspector, regretting every decision I had ever made, envisioning my brides humiliation.

Flower returned shamed and exhausted. She disappeared into the wooden chair beside me as I raked my fingers-nails down my face. Soon, I was in a room with no windows, pulling my own underwear down, lifting my nuts, blooming my ass.

They found nothing.

"Okay," the guard said. "Button up. Out to the car now."

Outside, they fingered through our belongings for ten minutes, opening every pocket of every bag, every coat, pairs of jeans, everything. Gripping Flower's waist, I thought back to my wedding day when I was crying into my friend's dress shirts. An orgy of love.

Now, I was ready to choke on new salty tears.

There I stood, almost passing out, when I saw the inspector go right into the sports bag where that last damn nub was. I knew he would find it. He'd be pissed that I lied. I also knew that it was a Saturday and we would be staying the weekend, riding this delicious slice of life out until Monday morning, the earliest.

My wife in one cell, myself in another.

Pretty picture, huh?

But then I saw the inspectors hand pull back and zip up the bag. Nothing. Holy fuck.

"Enjoy your honeymoon. You're free to go."

Steering the car through downtown Yarmouth, I was locked into a million emotions, my sensory on overload, exhausted. I wanted to pull over on the side of the road and dream this nightmare gone.

Flower was fast asleep in the front seat, out cold. Not a single sign of rage anywhere. Just the Canadian wind blowing through her hair, ruffling her now well-worn orange top.

Then, thirty miles down the road, after listening to the first side of John Mellencamp's "Scarecrow" on a cassette, everything felt right again. Just like it did back in college when I was in a jam and I needed someone, anyone, to have my back, no questions asked, Flower was there standing strong beside her man.

The experience at the border was traumatic. Horrifying, to say the least. Yet we endured, once again, together as one, from Day One.

She would walk on knives for me, I said to myself. As I would for her.

Next stop...Digby.

22. LIVING PROOF

She arrived in this world covered in love, and screaming so hard her little tongue shivered wildly as the nurses cleared her nose and throat of mucus. Born just five days before Christmas 2001, my daughter, Danielle, has managed to shake the foundation of my existence like nothing I've ever known.

The second act of my life has just begun. Danielle Jessica is playing the lead.

Throughout my wife's pregnancy, friends of mine described the birth of their children as "incredible," "monumental," "the most fantastic string of minutes ever imagined."

"I need that rush," I'd tell them. "I need that sense of astonishment that tears down old walls."

Admittedly, my spirituality had needed a tuneup. Lacking faith in all things that I don't know had been a common theme for 31 years. "Maybe this will wake me up," I thought. But witnessing Danielle's birth didn't feel the way I thought it would. I thought it would be groundbreaking, dramatic and mind alerting. Although my heart pounded straight out of my skin, no tears fell from my eyes when she made her entrance.

"You rotten stone!" I berated myself on the inside. Everything just went too fast. I couldn't get my footing.

In the delivery room, dressed in white coveralls and a paper-thin cap, I once again played the dunce of the classroom. As a busy hum of terminology filled the room, I felt like a fool, totally lost. I wouldn't say I was unappreciative of what was going on. I knew that by nine that same morning, I'd no longer be a boy. I'd be a father, a man.

Still, as Steinbeck once wrote, "Woman got all her life in her arms. Man got it all in his head."

My head was full.

I was too concerned for my wife, Flower, who lay on the gurney to my right. She was zoned out and confused, and her caesarean section still had to be sewn shut. Suddenly, I was looking down at a greasy little something that resembled a junior-sized Mr. Magoo. She was spectacular. Fully pink and covered in wrinkles, Danielle was my new life. Still, my eyes were dry as a bone.

When my wife got to the recovery room, she was as courageous as ever. Dripped out on Demerol with a six-inch incision across her belly, she managed to show her new baby just what love feels like.

"She's perfect," she said, holding Danielle tight to her chest.

That night, long after family and friends left the hospital, a minor breakdown occurred. My wife, still wobbly from the drugs, lay on the bed in a haze as Danielle fell into a perfect rage.

I changed her, rocked her, kissed her brow repeatedly-and still the crying continued. When a nurse came in the room to check my baby's vital signs, I left the hospital to get some air. Sitting in my truck in an empty parking lot in Saugus, I called my brother in California for some advice. "I'm not sure if I'm cut out for this," I told him. "I never even cried!"

In less than 10 minutes, my brother Mike explained that my reaction to the birth wasn't to be graded. "There is no right or wrong way to act," he said. "Just be yourself."

On the drive back to the hospital, I put on a Springsteen song called "Living Proof." In the song, he sings about long droughts before a hard rainfall. It was then I realized my role as a father wasn't to cry. It was to weather the storm of emotions entering into my heart and to be strong for my new family.

To be a man.

23. HEAVY SEVEN

There are those who say that life is made up of seven significant moments.

Like the seven Gateways to Payola, and the seven Bowls of Wrath, and the seven Angels of Mercy, the seven moments of life are there to provide answers to your accomplishments or front a mirror to your indecencies.

When I thought back to my own Heavy Seven, my skins began to shift, a pallor came to my wrists, my tongue began to braid itself. Hoops of visions began ducking back into my mind, my heart, multiplying in logic, dividing sin from salvation.

I wanted to beat most of the memories out of me.

Suddenly, I am 10-years-old, staring up at a poster of the "The Fonz" that hung on my bedroom wall. You see, to me, Fonzerelli always crushed Kowalski, and then he took his girl. The hard-working mechanic from Milwaukee with an eye on the prize, his brown leather jacket worn down to perfection, jeans well washed, hair on point, every gesture in place—the Fonz meant everything to me, every move he made, hug he gave, threat he waged on Potsie and Ralph was the antithesis of cool. And then some.

Then I found myself pinned into a rented bedroom. A counting crow sang of orange skies on the radio. Without work, a reasonable diet or a real reason for leaving the love of my life, I considered the unforgivable. Not for long, not even a moment. But the notion was there, and she was selling it hard.

My mind soon traveled to a summer on Cape Cod. I was hurling my bride around the dance floor, crying into my friend's pressed linen shirts, drunk on faith. Love so immense that even the marshes near by wept fat, salty tears.

Were these the visions of my Last Breath?

Soon, I envisioned a clear nirvana, a child sliding from her mother's womb. The power of this miracle released me. No "Hail Marys." No "Our Fathers." Just another good reason to shut the fuck up.

Now, I'm back in my early 20s, living at home with my mother, cold cuts at the ready. Half a man, bugged eyes, a face torn with grief, I took a job I learned to hate. Working through the moment, I honored my hours by reinventing myself, again. Then quit.

A ball game and a chain-linked fence. A schoolmate with a gnarly grin stares through the metal at me and says, "Look at you. Always on the wrong side of the fence." Beaten yet aware, I would learn to be a better friend and never stand alone again.

Christmas Eve at an Italian restaurant, wet, cold Boston night. An empty seat, a mangled heart and the holiday chatter is busting out all around me as the horror waits in the wings. Then, a wireless call, a hard ride up the interstate, and then—tears, shock and a Christmas spent in hell.

But I didn't want my reflections to end there, not at that place, not ever again. I wanted my mind to keep clicking, a night with twin redheads, coolers of beer, concert lights, home runs and better grades. I wanted that moment I could look back on and say, "Yup, right there. That's when I made it." But, it doesn't work that way. This we know, or ignore, or embrace.

It was then, as I plodded down the road in my oxygen truck, I wondered: What of my Gateway to Payloa? When will she offer me her loving loins?

I wrote that screed in one fell swoop one evening when I returned home from driving an oxygen truck all day. Barrelling into the house, limply nodding to my wife and kids as they stood in the kitchen, I was mouthing the words to myself—*There are those that say that life is made up of seven significant moments*—over and over again, just as I had been doing for the last 15 miles racing up Route 93 to put those words to paper.

That line first popped into my head somewhere near the New Hampshire border and I didn't want to lose it, not for anything. They weren't groundbreaking words, this I knew. But there was something in that sentence telling me it was time to get back into the writing game.

It had been ages since I had done anything to further my quest to be heard. I hadn't written a single word in four years. I was a new father, a crabby husband, and completely lost as we hemorrhaged money, feeling very much like a big old nothing all over again. How could that be? I had family, friends, and although completely broke, I even owned a home. Got to love the early 2000s!

Still, not since I rattled off a good fifty bylines writing for the *Boston Globe* over the course of a few years in the early 2000s, working as a correspondent, selling my stories to both the Home and Travel sections of the papers, I really hadn't done jack shit creatively since I was 32. And not that

I didn't remind myself of this reality every single day during those years. It ate away at me, the sheer gravity of this lethargy. I just didn't have any ideas left in my head. I was crisp, dried out, completely funkified.

During my more productive years, I wrote for the *Globe* and other publications like the *Improper Bostonian, Venue, Details, King, Ramp* and a handful of other "dude" magazines. I traveled to the middle of the Mississippi Delta to chase the Blues and wrote about it. I attended a swingers party on the North Shore of Boston and got a birds-eye view of what a sexy night of couples sharing really looks like (from a distance) and wrote about it. I followed the famous boxing promoter, Don King, around Las Vegas for three days, and wrote about how The Don worked his way around the ring in the hours leading up to a heavyweight championship bout. I drag raced my Honda Accord and stalled the transmission out on "Grudge Night" at a drag strip in New Hampshire and wrote about it, well enough to make it onto the cover of the *Boston Globe Magazine* one time. Those were good days, when I was flush with ideas, locking down writing gigs like it was nobody's business. And making some money at it, too.

Twenty seven jobs later, after graduating from college, I got into writing free for rock zines like "Z" in Boston, going to shows, writing reviews. You could always find a Z magazine at Stairway to Heaven, free on a rack. This was around 1996. It was a fantastic publication to figure out what kind of writer you wanted to be. Can you help make the band stand out? Can you entertain the reader? I did neither, but I felt a voice growing inside me, my own voice. I still hung on a bit too strong to the Rules of Gonzo, but I began to ease away from the Good Doctor, giving him the space he rightfully deserved.

Local papers maybe paid $25 for an article, and I sold a few. So many that I can't remember a single one. The "dude" rags, if you could ever get to an editor with a story idea, might score you $200 for a couple thousand words. And that would take months for you to receive, tied up in some startup bullshit. One time, for the drag racing piece in the *Globe*, I locked down $1,500 dollars for my efforts. For a hack like me—a broke-assed hack—that was amazing, a trip into uncharted waters. Fit with a full page spread, killer cover, pro photography, great editing, up to that point that cover story was my Mona Lisa.

And brother, it was worth blowing out the trannie on my Honda.

Then it all vanished into a pool of debauchery made up of chemical drugs and a gnawing sense of responsibility. "My shit's fucked up." Warren Zevon sings on his tremendous album, "Life'll Kill Ya." And it certainly was for me, too. Wrung out again, this time without any fight left in me, I was honeycombed, dumb as a wafter. Bills, kids, wife, wet basement, hernia, feeling ignored, forgotten, sorry for myself. A big mess once again.

Back in the day, when I found myself in a writer's funk, I would romanticize my ailing disposition until it came back strong again by reading more, talking less. But this was different. This was me alone in my bedroom once again, hiding beneath the sheets from my mother, terrified at my return to being a nobody.

Then, by the grace of God, those words shot into my head, *"There are those that say that life is made up of seven significant moments."* And just like that, the funk ended, and hasn't shown its face since.

I took to the Ice Box that night, skipping dinner, skipping tubby and story time, skipping every duty I was suppose to be doing as a doting father and instead I wrote and wrote until my jaded past scorched my broken memories. The words flowed out of me—fell out of me—like they'd been just sitting there waiting to be unleashed, freed from a constipated mind.

I'd never used, never heard or written the word "payola" in my life, but there she was, laid out before me, kissing me on the cheek, as if saying, "You're welcome, shitbrains." I had completely forgotten about that poster of the Fonz. Likely, not giving it a single thought since I took the poster down from my bedroom wall back in the early 1980s, soon after the Fonz, yes, "jumped the shark." Memories of my wedding day six years early, of course, were still there, though somewhat clouded by the intense celebration. As I wrote about that hot August day, my eyes filled with tears, thinking of my friends, my wife, my siblings, all the people that had given up their weekend to be on the Cape with us, bathing in this "orgy of love." Revisiting the chain link fence incident regurgitated all kinds of nauseating feelings. Feelings of weakness and isolation—damnation. I could still see that boy's face, his toothy grin, his indignation towards me, and I still want to eat that face. And when I thought back on that Christmas Eve when I barged into my father's condominium, yelling his name—"Dad! Dad! DAD!"—I could still see his terrorized eyes shoot wide open as I turned him over in his bed, certain he was dead.

When I was done, I knew those words were the best and most honest

I had ever written. Again, I wasn't trying to be Poe or Flannery or Hunter. They were my words, my confession, and I stood by them. They weren't crass like Spankin' It and I didn't need Elvis to shake his hips to reassure me of their importance. I knew those words would lead me in a new direction, but where?

It didn't really matter where. I had broken through, gotten past this stage of stagnation. That's about all I knew, that I was reinvigorated when I finished writing *Heavy Seven*, feeling the urge to write more and more. I took that piece and I sent it out everywhere—newspapers, magazines, even a few literary online sites, which were a new thing back then. No one was half as impressed as I was with my proclamation. Rejection, rejection, rejection. And you know what? I didn't care, not in the slightest. Undaunted, I knew I would need a thick burst of luck, a glowing bird, a loving figure full of goodwill to see the essays relevance. And when she did arrive, maybe a year or more after I wrote the piece, that glowing bird, that loving figure turned out to be my own big sister, Laura.

Years had past since Laura spit a loogie in my face or beat me senseless with her powerful legs. She was a longtime post production manager at WGBH-TV in Boston for shows like "Antique Roadshow" and she was also, as they say, somewhat "in the know." Laura had read a few of my newspaper articles in the past and, I think, she was mildly impressed. Other times when she read my writings, she simply thought I sounded like a dickhead. I mean, she worked with real pros—directors and writers and producers. Laura saw talent everyday, people with fresh ideas and real skills in the visual arts.

One of the directors she worked with was on a show called "*Fetch! With Ruff Ruffman*" is a man named Paul Serafini. Very accomplished, talented, extremely kind, a Daytime Emmy Award winning director, Serafini was also someone looking to direct his first film. This was before he manned the helm of his second film, the 2016 multi-million dollar production, *Annabelle Hooper and the Ghost of Nantucket*, a family mystery. You go, Paul!

My sister and Paul worked closely together and she ended up showing him a copy of Heavy Seven, knowing he was looking for some story to direct. Paul read it, enjoyed it, saw some life in it, and soon after I received an email from Paul inquiring whether I could turn this into a screenplay.

Reply: Of course I can, Paul. I'll send you something soon. Thanks, Rob.

That was bullshit. I had no idea how to write a screenplay. I could barely glue together a cohesive essay without drifting off into some fading tangent. Never in my life had I written a screenplay. I had dreamt of it, sure, yes indeed. Tarantino, Peckinpah, Scorsese, writers and directors like that, the movies they wrote, these guys were who I looked up too. They were complex geniuses that did all the dirty work for us, the movie-goer. They dared to swim in the dark waters of the mind, in violence, in rage, in lust and light. They worked with what they had and made gold out of it. Peeling back the layers of the human psyche, blood at the ready, these men had a vision and they stuck to it.

Soon after making a promise I didn't think I'd keep, I polished off a very weak screenplay version of Heavy Seven starring my father, Robert, as the lead, years after he began acting at age 57, a few years after he retired. He played a man named Bobby Merlot, someone looking back on the seven moments of his own life and the sins he carried with him. Careenging in and out of the character's adult life, going back as far as his adolescence, my father played the tragic hero like a champ. He knew this guy, his pains, his better days . . . and worst. Like some of the great filmmakers, my father was also a complex genius of sorts, someone that used what he was given in life and made the best of it.

Then, stretched its limits until it all burned to ash.

Over the course of two plus years, we chipped away at the short film. Laura produced and put up a good amount of the money for production costs, all while managing everyone's schedules and moods. We were on a stick-thin budget, but she approached the project as if it was readying it for submission to the Oscars. Gold standard stuff. Paul worked his way around shooting a scene with the patience of a saint, always positive, calm, ready for the next best take. He had a great eye, and the compassion he bestowed upon the crew only enhanced his skills and willingness to go deeper to catch that perfect moment in a frame. We had a cast of characters that came from various backgrounds in acting. From real pros to first timers. It was a mash up of performances, all good, some better than others, and some, well, were just incredible. Like Bobby Merlot.

When the film was completed and ready be shown to a crowd of invited guests at a theater in Harvard Square, I couldn't help but be blown away by the event. Never did I figure on this happening, my words being acted out on the big screen, heard by a theater full of people. Scary shit.

Of course, this wasn't Hollywood, and we never made into the Aspen Film Festival. Al Pacino's manager never reached out to play Bobby Merlot in the sequel to Heavy Seven. And I never strove to reach those heights in my ambitions. It was all in the chase, the fear, the willingness to believe in those little ideas that come to you in life and simply utilize them. They arrive for a reason, this I am certain. Then, once caught, you cage that fear and get it ready for breeding.

My quest was complete. It took over 20 years to reach these minimal heights. The rejections, the creeping doubts, the narcissistic nights and bottomed out days, they were all part of the process. Now, the only thing there was to do was to keep going, start working on something new. When a business man makes his first million he doesn't rest his hat on that wad and say, "Nah, I'm good. That's enough." No! He starts working on making his next million.

So, I went to work. But first, I went to Asbury Park in search of The Boss.

24. THE JERSEY FLASH PART I

It's not easy for a grown man to admit he spent a weekend in November hunting down his boyhood hero off the Garden State Parkway. There's something slightly obsessive about the image.

But I did just that. The Stone Pony, a rock club in Asbury Park, New Jersey, was hosting the "Light of Day" concert benefiting the Parkinson's Disease Foundation. Two friends and I headed down, hoping against hope that Bruce Springsteen would be there.

My friends Johnny Boy and Big Joe and I, all loyalists to the midnight hour and eager to be freed from the sullen grind of a working life, came to the shore barely containing our expectations, seeking a rare encounter of the strangest kind. Knowing such Jersey legends as Joe Grushecky and the Houserockers, the Stone Caravans, Jobonanno and the Godsons of Soul, and rhythm and blues artist Gary U.S. Bonds would be performing was reason enough to pay the oft-maligned Jersey Shore a visit. But when I mentioned to the guys that there was a slight chance Springsteen would drive down from his estate in Rumson, a few miles from Asbury Park, they granted me the wheel.

Rumors had swirled for months that Springsteen, then a young 55, would make a cameo at the benefit. Fresh off the Vote for Change Tour in support of presidential candidate John F. Kerry, he was said to be in town, percolating. Springsteen had shown up at each of the four previous Light of Day shows at the Stone Pony, usually popping in around midnight, when the action inside was hot. We were hoping for a cool fifth.

We arrived in Asbury Park around 6 that night. It was dark. The ocean was out there somewhere. We could smell it. But we couldn't take our eyes off the rubble. Half-built high-rises surrounded by trash held our attention. Spray-painted faces on chipped concrete walls had us thinking, "What happened here?"

Back in the 1930s, when Asbury Park (population 16,930 in 2000) was flourishing, world-renowned performers, trade and street shows, carnivals and conventions filled the boardwalk. Life was about paddle boats and big white hats, lacy dresses and massive wooden Victorian homes encased in angles and points. Things deteriorated after World War II. Fires burned out buildings. Air travel became more affordable, enough so that residents could leave the boardwalk behind and vacation away from home. The city soon fell apart.

Those days, merchants, townsfolk, politicians, and performers from Asbury Park were all doing their part to breathe new life into the city. Trendy restaurants with ethnic cuisine were springing up. Galleries featuring artists from around the globe sit across from coffee shops and bistros. The buildings were power washed.

We drove down Ocean Avenue, past a small structure on the corner of Second Street with "Stone Pony" on the awning. "It'll all happen in there," I said. Joe's mind shifted. "We'll need a good base," he said, suggesting clams casino, fried calamari, and rib-eye steak as a stomach liner. Minutes later, we were pouring glasses of merlot at La Nonna Piancone's Cafe on Main Street in Bradley Beach, south of Asbury.

Over dinner, we discussed how tired we were of stories about people meeting former Boston Celtics player Larry Bird in a discount store or seeing author Norman Mailer at a muffler shop. We wanted our moment. "He's out there somewhere," John said, sniffing a forkful of beef. "I can smell him."

The next morning, having stayed at a decent but depressing motel in Neptune, we moved our bags to the Empress Hotel on the boardwalk in Asbury Park. We could see the Stone Pony just blocks from our balcony. The sea looked cold, but our sheets were clean and the sun was bright.

For the next six hours we strolled the boardwalk. There was a Civil War reenactment taking place on the beach. Tents filled the grassy knoll near the fish pier. Reenactors in knee-high black boots signed phony treaties as mothers walked the city strip. We cased the Berkeley Carteret Oceanfront Hotel and Conference Center down near the Casino and Convention Hall, designed by Charles Wetmore and Whitney Warren, the same architects responsible for New York's Grand Central Terminal. The hotel has been there 65 years and was requisitioned as a service station for the Royal British Navy at the onset of the World War II.

Farther along, we passed Madame Marie's fortune parlor, a fixture on the boardwalk since 1932 and immortalized in the Springsteen classic, "4th of July, Asbury Park." The tiny block building was painted blue with Day-Glo lettering. Madame Marie was gone for the day, but there was a number on the door to call. So I called it.

When the ninety something Madame Marie answered, she told me to come to her home, only 3 miles away. I could have a reading done for $25, she said. "Are you catching any vibe about me over the phone?" I asked her, trying to snake my way out of spending the cash.

"Yes," she said. "You're a negative person and hard to make happy." I said goodbye to the Madame, thanking her for the brutal insight while my spirits were still intact and snapped my phone shut.

We then drove the shore looking for other landmarks.

We saw the famous clown painted atop The Wonder Bar, a scary-looking thing with a gummy grin. We wanted to swing open the same casino doors Springsteen had in his video for "Tunnel of Love." We found the doors, we think, but the old Ferris wheel in the video was gone, like so many things from Asbury's past.

Later, at Harry's Roadhouse on Cookman Avenue, we ordered meatloaf sandwiches. There was a lot of night ahead of us. If Springsteen were to show, it would be long after dark. Maybe even morning. So we sipped a few Guinnesses and measured the possibilities. We would give anything to see Springsteen up close. I'd seen him in arenas, music halls, and athletic centers, but never close enough to make out the folds around his eyes. We were born into his music, flush with his themes. We imagined Springsteen shuddering the same way if he were to cross paths with Hank Williams on the boardwalk, coming out of Madame Marie's.

By 8 p.m., we were showered and sprayed down, ready for the night. Our adjoining rooms at the Empress were perfect. The bathrooms held good steam and we could see if a line was gathering at the Stone Pony. No line. When we walked in a half hour later, the Stone Pony was slamming. Jobonanno and the Godsons of Soul were killing the packed house. There were over 200 people in the place, drinking in the deep rhythms. Under the pavilion outside the bar, conversations grew out of anxiousness. At one point, the once relaxed "We see him all the time" attitude dispensed by locals came to a halt. A very excited Asbury girl hanging out in the smoking section couldn't keep her emotions in check. "He's back there near the soundboard! I just saw!"

Who was "him," I wondered, and did she really mean it? My head rotated three times in my efforts to see Springsteen perched somewhere in that bar. Then, the roar went stage left and I saw Springsteen rolling past his people. Dressed in matching denim shirt and pants, he looked like an icon should: rakishly wise and humble, rested and lean. He cast a shadow 10 miles wide.

He took to the small stage with his friend and leader of the Houserockers, Joe Grushecky, a teacher from Pittsburgh. They rattled off classic heaters like "Murder Inc.," "Code of Silence," and "Light of Day." Then Springsteen, now soaked through his denim, played "Johnny 99," "This Hard Land," and "Atlantic City"—the songs saved for the lucky ones, for the E Streeters filling every inch of the bar.

Two hours later, Bruce was gone, but on the sidewalk outside the Stone Pony, people were shoulder to shoulder, asking about the night, making sure the last 90 minutes had, in fact, taken place.

Four nights later, back in Manchester, N.H., my head was still spinning. I couldn't get the night out of my head. I had seen the folds around his eyes, the gray in his sideburns, even the pores in his nose. I had been unearthed, Jersey style.

25. GIVING THANKS

Every year I wish my buddy T-Bone a "Happy Saint Patrick's Day" he says the same thing to me: "Bobby, I'm Irish every day of the year."

His terseness is honorable if not somewhat annoying, but I understand what Big Hoss was saying. He was letting me know that one's heritage and religion or race doesn't need to come packaged and sold in order to recognized.

I get it. Sweet of him to jam it down my throat.

But I remind Big T that reflection is a celebration in itself. We need it as humans, those rarified moments during the year when we're forced to admit our thanks to the world. Whether it's to the gods at Christmastime or a pile of punch drunk friends during Thanksgiving or to that weekend lover you hustled onto the legion hall dance floor on Valentine's Day, giving thanks is a healthy gesture.

And those on the receiving end of that appreciation can only feel warmth upon acceptance.

That's why I give thanks to the opportunities music has given me and bow down to all the dealers, the ones feeding me the junk, the funk, the folk and cow punk and thank them properly for their dirty deeds done so sweet.

Their music has shaped my life, given me a voice, given me access to some of the most gifted writers and musicians of all ages—men, women and children—from all around New Hampshire and beyond.

These are the people that dictate my various and often frightening dispositions. Their minds and fingers and voices are that driving force behind my need to be enlightened, to be freed—at times—from my own quest to be heard.

Without music, I'd be dead. On the inside at least. I don't crave a bagel in the morning and I don't eat yogurt. What I want in the morning is a piping hot cup of coffee and some music to "Kick starts my heart" that slaps the day into gear, work on making it a good one.

Music does that for me. Most days it breaks off chunks of aggression and allows me to witness what true passion sounds like in strings and verse right before my eyes. It's my fix, my temptress, my forever friend that's almost always there when needed most.

My friend Russ posted on Facebook once that music "got me through the darkest times and was always there to enhance the good days. All my favorite memories are triggered by the music I was listening to at the time."

He's right. Music doesn't eat at your innards like happy pills do. It lubes our senses on a three-minute loop and all that sweet grease of sound helps the darkness to slide right off. It never lasts because tomorrow comes with all her troubles. But music is always there to save you from your ruinous self if you just let her in.

I'm overwhelmed with thanks to WKXL 103.9 FM, WMNH 95.3 FM and New England College in Concord and WMNH in Manchester for allowing me to feed my quest to be heard on my weekly and monthly shows that feature live in-studio performances by artists from around the state.

I'm thankful that *The Concord Monitor* and *Manchester Ink Link* offer me my 800-word weekly space to blather on about all the great people making great music in this beautiful state. See, I get to sit back and watch these songwriters from the lakes, the seacoast, the city and mountains to touch down on brilliance week after week, going far beyond the boundaries of the normal mind.

Usually, I have no idea who I am meeting when they arrive in studio. Some have the look of an artist, some of a pipe fitter. Few carry an air about themselves. Some are rough, others oil smooth, but in the end none of that matters because there's beauty in all imperfections.

I'm blessed.

Courage is what I think of most when I think of all the musicians I've met over the years. The quiet drummer in the back, tapping the brushes, at peace, for now, while he's locked into the groove. Or the love-sick wounded angel who appears in your studio one night and sings her heart out about faded love and a craving for order. Or that unassuming gem of a musician who shows up built like a school boy but then lashed out into something mad and criminal.

For that and so much more, I give thanks to all of you for helping to beat back the darkness and bring light to this wicked, divided world.

26. BELKNAP COUNTY BLUES

The last time I was in the Belknap County Jail in Laconia, I was visiting my roommate from college, who, instead of breaking down kegs of beer with us on the weekends, left on Friday afternoons to become just another inmate at the county jail. That was part of his sentence for his stupidity, weekends in jail for an entire semester, then a longer stint when the school year ended.

That was over 20 years ago.

So, when a musician I met named Dr. Jack Polidoro from Belmont mentioned that he and some other musicians would be playing a special concert for the inmates at Belknap in a few days, I jumped at the chance to get back inside. Yes, Johnny Cash's famous live prison concert album, "Folsom Prison Blues" played into my curiosity. But I didn't expect to see a recreation of the historic 1968 event. I was curious to see if the spirit of Cash would reappear in the clouds gathered round the pink sunset that hung over the barbed wired bullpen area.

As the first batch of minimum security female inmates made their way into the pen, each in matching green prison garb, it didn't take but five seconds to see the elation in their smiling faces. Not just because they were outside breathing clean air on a gorgeous summer night.

Because they were being treated to something other than their own bad luck.

It was a pedicure of sorts, minus the toe rub.

The women came in all ages and sizes, some young, still sporting a flowing lock of highlighted hair, others carrying a hard-lined expression that made them a perfect fit for this joint.

Then the men came into the yard, twenty of them, and they appeared equally thankful to be freed from the choking scent of incarceration.

And like men do, they played the hard guy as they took their seats next to the ladies, who, like women, pretended the men sitting five-feet next to them didn't even exist.

It was starting to feel like a real mixer.

Rob and Patsy, an older hippy couple played some great old hippy tunes. And knowingly or not, the inmates, who I doubt rocked out to the "Mamas and the Papas" before they did the deed that got them done, seemed to know ever line to Bob Dylan's "Make You Feel My Love."

And when Percy Hill and Leon Garretson started singing about Whisky Mama and daddy's deep deviled blues, well, everyone seemed to settle into the night, forgetting about where they were, how they got there or when and if they'd ever get out.

They knew this song cold. And felt it.

As the pink sky disappeared into the foothills, Dr. Jack took the stage and delivered the perfect song on a perfect night to the perfect audience, "Pancho and Lefty" by Townes Van Zandt.

Livin' on the road my friend
Is gonna keep you free and clean
And now you wear your skin like iron
And your breath is hard as kerosene

Some of the inmates sat rubbing their neck, patiently sitting through the performances. Others grabbed for the spotlight, giving it their best to make an impression on the ladies by shouting louder than the other inmates. Just being their goofy selves. Like anyone.

Pastor Deb played and she was special. There was something about the way the men and women looked at Deb as she sang that made them shed their angry skin. As if Deb was, maybe, the only person in the world they could trust and believe in. And while Pastor Deb belted out the chorus to the "4 Non Blondes" major hit, "What's Going On?" everyone in the bullpen sang loud and proud, as if they were in the midst of a kitchen jam with a bunch of friends and plenty of libations and nothing but love for one another.

Locked into the moment, I could have wept.

Sitting in a folding chair in the front row, an inmate named Tyler, maybe 40, strong, black and seemingly kind, listened hard to the quiet songs about screwing up and digging your way out. He threw his arms out wide when a song about beating the odds emerged. Tyler has been in county for the past six months, still waiting on a court date for whatever he did. But tonight, as Tyler said, "is the best thing that's happened to me since I been in jail. It's really blowing my mind."

Yup, music will ease a troubled mind.

As will freedom.

27. LET'S MAKE A MOVIE

Over the course of seven years, I wrote five more short films. Some I produced, some I even directed myself. "Muddy," "Candles in Paradise," "Bingo," "Overdrawn" and "De Facto Inc." They all varied in quenchability. "Muddy" was the best, not only because it won "Best of the Festival" at the SNOB Film Festival in Concord NH., by beating out more than 60 other films. It just felt so right. "Candles in Paradise" broke my heart, sending me into exile from my own hometown. "Bingo" was shot with three stage comedians making up their own lines as we went along. I would give these hungry New Hampshire comics, each on a quest of their own, the scene, the setting, and off they went into a maze of hilarity, making it up on the fly. "Overdrawn" was full of unresolved resentments and "De Facto Inc" was straight up pulp.

Each summer, for a half dozen years, me and a small crew of filmmakers set off and make one very short film, something that's cooked up on a shoestring budget, always searching for that perfect beat.

And we work hard to line those beats up, as a musician does, or even a painter or poet. The scenes, like a verse or stanza, must flow, must encompass a steadiness that keeps the viewers from checking Facebook, turning the dial, walking out of the theater. Or even rewriting the entire scene themselves. And, like any kind of work, some days you got it, some days you don't. That flow we speak of is so elusive, so cunning and distant. She wants to be chased, wants to be considered not once but a 1000 times a day.

But to hunt for flow is one thing. To clutch her is another.

So, one Sunday, I walked into Modern Gypsy vintage store in Manchester to film the final scene of this summer's project, called De Facto Inc, and I was a total disaster, unfit to lead a shoot let alone lock down any kind of flow.

My brain was dead from an emotional week. My mother had brain surgery. My father-in-law was fighting through a bout of spinal meningitis. I'd lashed out terribly at someone I loved. And I was seven days into sulking about Mother Nature raining on our music festival the previous weekend.

Boo-hoo, right. Welcome to Life.

But then Tajoura arrives on set, a beautiful African American actress who drove up from NYC to shoot this ridiculously pulpish scene based off redemption and lust. We'd never met and I'm sure she was impressed with my lifeless gaze and flow-less demeanor. Poor gal was about to do a passionate makeout scene with an actor she's never met named Curtis Lanciani, and, like a true professional, she was rolling with the punches more than I was.

And what did I really have to do besides say, "Action!" Not much.

But then, just before our cameraman Chris Tremblay turns to me and says, "We're ready," flow gracefully arrives at the front door of the thrift shop smelling like old shirts and a half empty pouch of tobacco.

Delicious.

It was then I knew how musicians must feel when a producer signals from the control room, "Okay. Hit it, Roy." All those months of picking, writing and preparation that led up to these few short hours of recording did actually mean something. The mind's eye would finally pay witness to the imagination.

The scene unravels and the actors, after several tweaks and edits and repositioning, have started to warm up to each other. Their lines were beginning to mesh. Tajoura started to tug at Curt's shirt with a little more authority than earlier. Between shots, Curt dabbed at a bead of sweat on her forehead, revealing the soft side of the man she is about to devour as they stumble backwards in heat.

Meanwhile, I am just trying to keep the pace, making sure the pockets of silence between the lines don't run wild. I'm chanting on the inside, thinking of the audience, "Harness, secure, deliver." Still, I have never shot a love scene for a film. Sadly, never been in one either. But this scene calls for Curt and Tajoura to attack each other in passion. And flow or no flow, I wanted to see this!

Each take was superb with the actors conjuring up an animalistic flow of desire. They fell through a line of hanging ties into a cluttered backroom—grasping, kissing, flowing throughout the 15 second shot. It was perfect.

Yet, I insisted on calling from behind Chris' shoulder again and again, "Cut. Do it again. Cut. Again. Cut. One more time." Until finally Chris throttled me over the head with a sound pole and said,. "I think we got the shot."

"Not without Flow we won't," I say. "Nothing works without her."

28. VISITING THE HOME OF HUNTER S. THOMPSON

"Buy the ticket, take the ride."

So, we did.

All the way to Woody Creek, Colo., on the weekend of Independence Day, 2017. Myself, my brother and a good friend flew to Denver, then drove three and a half hours through the Rockies, not in search of a parade, or a mountain, or even to witness a single firework flash through the star-studded skies.

No, sir.

Instead, we opted to stand in the kitchen of the late Dr. Hunter S. Thompson's home at "Owl Farm" and drink good whisky while listening to his wife, Anita, and longtime friend, former Pitkin County sheriff, Bob Braudis, tell hilarious and frightening tales of the famous writer's fondness for firearms, how he loved to see his own byline, his struggles with aging and his fierce devotion to his readers.

All this as we wandered his home freely, bathing in the spirit of the Good Doctor.

If you've followed Thompson's work since his book Hell's Angels back in 1967, then you know the legend of Dr. Hunter S. Thompson. He was a really great writer that blended comedic prose with hardcore journalism and flipped the literary world on its head with books like Fear and Loathing in Las Vegas and The Great Shark Hunt. His writing was wild, his life even wilder. He was a wrecking ball of sorts, a force of nature with a southern man's sensibilities and a rock-and-roll persona.

The trip was wrapped around "Wild Fest 2017," a "communal bash" featuring bands and good beer set on Thompson's vast acreage of property, just a few miles outside Aspen. I love a festival and the view was stoic beyond compare. But I wasn't there for the music or the summer snow caps.

I wanted into Hunter's home, into the very place where he perfected "gonzo journalism" and wrote all that stinging commentary about the death of the American Dream. I wanted to lean against the same countertop that steadied the backs of such righteous dignitaries as Bob Dylan, Warren Zevon, Keith Richards and countless other twisted outsiders. I wanted to smell the history in the throw rugs, touch the spines of the books that lined the walls of his living room, taste the water under the kitchen sink spigot and sit at the desk where Hunter fired off so many unforgettable lines that burned to conquer and corrupt.

The tour was part of a package, the "Gonzo Package" as it was called, and the money helped fund Wilderness Workshop, a nonprofit. You could tack on a small fee of $50 to the festival's ticket price and take part in the first ever official tour of Hunter Thompson's home. I jumped at the opportunity, the three of us did. My mind's eye has recreated this scenario in color for 27 years, ever since I read the words Hunter wrote, "We were somewhere around Barstow on the edge of the desert when the drugs began to take hold."

We stood on Hunter's front porch, feet away from his famous 1971 Chevy Impala parked in the driveway. There it was. The Red Shark. Crazy. I was nervous, quiet, wondering if what I see inside would match my dreams. Would the counters now be granite? His desk roped off? The tour was scheduled for only 20 minutes. Lots to process in that time.

Ten disciples of Hunter's from Utah, San Diego and the Granite State were greeted by our gracious host, Anita, and she looked nervous herself. After all, this was the first time she's allowed the public officially into her home, into a shrine built by her husband, a man of many letters.

Sheriff Bob arrived soon after and we went inside to Hunter's living room and stood around the same heavy wooden coffee table and brick fireplace that I've seen in documentaries for years, enjoying a bowl of Colorado's finest. There were no ropes, no guards, just a maddening amount of images to ingest before our time was up. Books and paintings, photographs and pins, bottles and green visors. Seemingly thousands of conversations, declarations, violations were baked into the walls of that room.

Anita then welcomed us into the kitchen, Hunter's work room. It was masterfully cluttered, a wonderful maze of affirmations, from the couch to the TV to the American flag hooked to the frame of a window near his desk. There was a density to this kitchen that was shrouded in anguish and adulation. A place where poets, police and politicians could endure.

"Untouched," Anita said of the kitchen, since Hunter's death in 2005, with the exception of the chair where he ended things for good.

At Hunter's desk, inches away from the IBM typewriter where he wrote such powerful prose, shot glasses were laid out before a bottle of Chivas, the author's favorite whisky. Anita poured us each a glass and we raised it, toasted the Duke and stayed an hour longer than the tour allotted. Sheriff Bob stretched out on the couch and made us all cramp with laughter. Anita mothered us through the moment, providing unconditional acceptance and some deep cut snapshots into the writer's life.

Finally, I asked Anita if I could sit at Hunter's desk. It had taken me nearly three decades to do so. "Of course you can," she said without hesitation. I positioned myself behind the typewriter, looked down at the keyboard, at the numerous convention lanyards and reading glasses, the air spray and pack of cigarettes and my mind was blown, a flurry of humility rushed over me.

We had bought the ticket, we took the ride, now it was time to go home, fat with memories.

Mission accomplished. Check please!

29. WHO ARE THESE PEOPLE?

I once received an email from a reader of mine that said, "When I read your columns I feel completely lost. Who are these people? What are their sounds?"

Valid questions.

And I know where you're at, thinking wise. Maybe feeling a bit beyond the fence, somewhere just out of earshot of that sweet-tasting, blood-burning music you been reading about...but never seen live.

Not a problem. There are ways to remedy this.

First things first: Do you own a car? Good, then hit the road. Don't worry about the cats, the kids, the nine hours of sleep you require or the lack of flat backs in your pocket. Just focus on where you want to marinate in the music for a few hours.

Do you like the Lakes Region? The White Mountains? The grizzled streets of Manchester? Maybe your tastes lean toward them border towns where the metal bands bring the shine. These are all viable options, all teeming with great musicians and all kinds of sounds.

So, what are you thinking? Do you wish to see men play a jawbone, a fiddle, a relic banjo and learn about the Civil War at the same time? You can do that. "The Hardtacks" might be playing at any given library or music hall from Laconia to Salem.

Let's punch them up on Google. Click Hardtacks. Click Calendar. Bang. Write it down, set the clock and bingo, you're ready to be entranced, enlightened and engaged. OK you want to pass on the jawbone. It's an acquired taste, sure. But you love the blues and how it makes your coffee taste and how fun driving is with B.B. at your side, but you really want to see the blues performed live, pinched faces, thick knuckles and all.

Thankfully, you won't have to go far. Again, hit Google, punch in Arthur James, Delanie Pickering or Baza Blues from New Hampshire and off you go. That cup of coffee will come back hard into your face once

Mr. James gets to ripping on his pink guitar. Delanie? Yup, buckle up, sister. One whiff off her golden pipes and you will figure out her sound real quick.

Not much into the bar scene you say? Ok, well, you're not alone. I once was a lone wolf, too, scared of my own shadow, convinced my social skills had gone to rot.

Still, my shadow and pride were pulling at me from side-to-side. Then I looked around and said to myself, "Get up, hoss, and get out of yourself. Nobody gonna bite ya."

You asked, "Who are these people?" Well, you won't find them in Good Housekeeping or on Fox News or moonlighting on Game of Thrones. You'll find these influential, multi-talented, swagger-soaked musicians in all corners of the state, armed to the teeth with gear and passion.

They're teachers, cameramen, moms, craftsmen, grandfathers, farmers, businessmen and vagabonds doing the work that makes our hearts beat to perfection and our heads swim with hope.

They've put years (sometimes decades) of practice into their art, daily exercises of the body and mind, and they do it all, as Townes Van Zandt sang, "for the sake of the song."

That's who they are.

But in the end, my dear, it's all on you. Don't expect the music to come knocking on your front door. It's out there, blazing a vicious path these days all across the Granite State.

But the music isn't going to chase you.

You must chase the music.

30. FLOAT, MOM, FLOAT

It week was a terrible week, a beautiful week, a week full of strife and wonder.

My mother, only 78 — but a good, full 78 — was diagnosed with the Big C, and holy hell, shit moved much too quick. Hospice, just three days after she had summoned her four adult children to our hometown of Melrose to let us know that something was definitely not right with her. She knew she was sick. But how sick?

I've seen my mother laid out flat in more than a few hospital beds for this-or-that ailment. Never once did I think she wasn't going to get out of that bed. In the past, even after having a tumor removed from her brain, my mother would have three loads of laundry done and the living room vacuumed four hours after being discharged.

Not this time.

For the first time, maybe ever, I saw a look in her eyes that I'd never seen before. Fear. Stone cold fear. The kind that leaves your heart pounding and short of breath, the tips of your fingers icy. Her mind was rattling, balancing a thousand thoughts, trying to focus on what she wanted when she goes. Ashes to ashes, a wake for her many friends, closure for her four children, ten grandchildren and baby Thomas, the great grandson. Just like the first grandson, aces all the way.

Deciding which funeral home to hold the services at is one thing. Dealing with the present is another. My mother was in grave condition, tied up on the insides, unraveling on the outside. She needed to be treated at a hospital, to be told exactly how—give or take—long does she have to live. This woman was a planner, you see. Always was. "Five means 4:30. And get that look off your face." Impossibly organized.

In the hospital my mother was informed she was at Stage 3 and could go through rounds of chemo and surgery, or finish out her beautiful life surrounded by an army of loved ones, comfortably numb at a hospice house on the north shore. She quickly chose the later. Not an easy decision for her, or anyone, dealing with the end, I'm sure. She wanted to be old, real old. Ninety-plus old, like her own mother was when she died. She had plenty of good dinners left in her. She had just purchased a new chair for her living room in Florida. She had a ton of friends she spoke to daily over a hot cup of coffee. Damn, and she'd loved her fruit.

Admittedly, my mother had lost most of her kick. She was small as a bird now, and weighted even less. And although she put her best face on each day, dismissing the fact that her energy was sapped due to her chronic COPD, for the first time since she was a kid, my mother started taking naps after lunch. Long ones, too, she said. She told no one about these midday slumbers, not ever, not before she was just days away from entering Kingdom Come. Too proud. I get it. She knew her brand and honored it. So be it.

Gone were the mind games. It had been nearly a decade since my mother and I had any sort of dust up. We spoke on the phone a couple times a month, and we saw each other a few times a year. She was tight with my wife and daughter, and she thought my son was hilarious. Just a sweet young man, sensitive like his old man. And this method of communication worked for us. I removed myself from the vortex, and due to that, we never got along better. No longer did I measure myself by my mother's once pentrating phrase: *Who do you think you are? You're damn right you're nobody.* I didn't care anymore. In fact, I knew she was proud of what I had accomplished with my local writings, radio and short films. She was maybe my biggest fan. I heard it in her voice when she would call after reading something in the paper I had written, and I knew she was genuinely happy—and maybe a bit surprised—that I had turned my bullshit into a reality. And I loved her for it, because, in the end, I was never really trying to impress my father or my brother, my friends or my teachers. I just wanted my mother to look at me with a touch of pride, to know that her son turned out to be more than just a nobody, a filthy nothing. It was a tough take-off, sure, with a ton of rejection, self-sabotage and plenty of fear along the way, but she celebrated my victories alongside me, and I felt it. I was more than a nobody to her. At least until her departure.

So, all that is pretty ugly, right? Death sucks. Life rules, all of it, even those tricky weeks when every wall seems to be crashing down on your back. Like my mother was having. Yet, through all this, something transformative had taken place within our family, somehow making us all love each other even more than we already do, which is pretty intense overall. It quite literally takes us a good 45-minutes to say goodbye to each other after a simple barbeque. We are huggers. And we kiss, and we tell each other we love each other, always. Cousins and nephews, nieces, brothers, girlfriends, hairy husbands and wives, doesn't matter. You're getting a kiss. You're going to feel the love.

Over the course of a week, I was humbled to witness my mother's courage, her unwillingness to fold, to shut it all down and whimper away into the night. Like I had done days earlier when I feel into her arms as she laid in her hospital bed, crying. "This is just too fast, Ma. I mean, what the fuck?"

"I know, honey." she said with tears in her eyes. "I didn't see this coming either."

We pulled ourselves together, turned over a rock or two, and I leaned down and put my face to her cheek and held it there, like I hadn't done in 40-years. I'll never forget that moment, the smell of her cheek, so clean and smooth. I should have done that more often. Stupid.

I was humbled by the decency of my mother's ten grandchildren, the sheer admiration and unconditional love they had for this woman. I mean, I knew they loved her, I just never knew how much they loved her. Astronomically! My nephew reached out to a manicurist he knew and got his "Nan" treated to a sweet shine on her blades. My niece, Meg, knowing her grandmother never liked looking anything but near perfect, washed and bathed her, dried and fluffed her hair, prepping her for a full day of visitors. I stand in awe of both women, the best of friends.

Every kid in our tribe, from their teens to 30's, made their way up Route 128, heading towards the water, visiting their grandmother multiple times. Eye-to-eye contact, real sharing, honest talks, cell phones on silence. They each rose beyond my expectations and my heart hurts with pride.

It's a funny thing, for years, when I thought of that day coming, I would have insisted on some answers from my mother. Not anymore. I didn't need answers. Didn't want them. What I needed was more time with my mother. More hand holding, more unrushed banter, more of this genuine love that lives, not within us, but outside of us when the it's flowing that deep.

So, float, Mom, float on this sea of love. We will all be swimming right beside you.

Right to the end.

31. THE JERSEY FLASH PART 2

This is a tale of raw stupidity. So, with that, I'll get right into it.

Because I'm a Bruce Springsteen cultist, as mentioned earlier, I decided a few years back to leave the sweet bosom of New Hampshire for one day only and hit the Jersey Shore. Out of that fever and a well-developed hunch-meter hatched over 30-years of tailing Mr. Springsteen, I rallied a buddy from Manchester and my brother for an all-out road trip to Asbury Park, New Jersey in search of The Boss.

I'm 48 now and should be embarrassed (I'm not) that I would still go through such lengths to track the 68-year old songwriter down on an off-night near his home, where Bruce might pop into a bar for a drink and end up playing with the house band for an hour and half.

It does happen. I witnessed it.

To me, Springsteen is that long-lasting impression that grabbed hold of me at age 15 and still won't let up on my fat neck. I really don't know how I'd answer if someone offered me 30-minutes of facetime with either Bruce or Jesus. I'd likely extend my hand to the bearded savior and say, "Well, I really do hope I get to see you again someday." Then shout, "Bruce! Hold up!"

When we reached Asbury Park, the atmosphere on the boardwalk only solidified my boss intuitiveness. I could feel it, smell it. He was out there somewhere. Our decision to abandon the Granite State for one day was dead on. The Wild Rover will be there tomorrow, we said, as will our wives, children and work.

Bruce may not.

The night was falling into place. Alejandro Escovedo, a terrific rocker from Austin, Texas, was booked to play the Stone Pony that night. Escovedo, who was out supporting his 2010 'Street Songs of Love' album, is worth the five-hour trek to see play all by himself. He's a slick dresser, great writer with a voice and style all his own.

Escovedo and Mr. Bruce, who lives just up the road in Monmouth County, had collaborated on a few songs during those years, and my gut said Bruce would be showing up at the Pony this night—late probably, almost at closing—and rip a few gems out with his buddy Alejandro.

The night progressed. Lots of hopeful chatter about possibility and chance took place. In-and-out of the Pony we walked throughout Alejandro's set. I needed to taste that ocean air, to stare long and hard down the Jersey boardwalk to complete the experience.

The body language on the doorman outside the Pony showed acceptance towards us, almost as if he knew why were were there, and, without inquiring, nor caring, he let us come and go.

"Just show the wristbands when you come back in," he said a few times. Simple stuff.

Oh, Escovedo was killing it inside the small club. We were maybe twenty feet from the famed stage, hurling them back, watching the skinny Texan do his thing. The energy was swallowing the crowd up. And everyone was feeling what we were feeling. Bruce!!!

Escovedo played a couple more song. It's was late in the evening and the beer was starting to taste tighter on the tongue. My buddy and I decide to step outside for some more "fresh air" and rip a joint before The Bossman showed. One last time burn and then we will really be cooking on the inside when the action takes off, primed and ready. Then, let the gods take over. I shouted to my pal standing near the sea wall.

"I can smell him, man." I said. "He's here."

He tapped out, we turned around, both wrists up, respecting bar law and headed into to see Bruce up close. But then a new face appeared before us at the door, something broken and loveless and thick with hate.

"No one's coming in," the monster informed us. "Not happening, guys."

"But I got the wristband, man!" I cried, posed as Wonder Woman.

"Doors are closed. Sorry."

Loathe that word!

Somewhere a father drops an easy homerun ball in front of his son. A bride faints at the altar. A heart stops beating. With little pride left, I bribed the doorman with my 1999 Hyundai.

"No thanks," he said with a gross grin.

Inside, the club began to swell, I could feel it, taste it, that power behind the applause, the unleashing of raw allegiance to one Man and his craft. I was blown backwards by the reverberations coming from inside the Pony. Bruce was now onstage! The crowd was losing its mind, shouting, "Bruuuuuuuce!"

I begged onto the beast, "I came all the way down from New Hampshire! Please! Please!"

"From where?" You fucker!

Half-hour later, around the time Bruce and Alejandro were tearing into a cover of the Rolling Stone's "Beast of Burden," I'm face down in my pillow at the hotel, dejected as if I just got a DWI. I prayed to be mindswept. I tried to shower. Tried to eat myself to sleep. Nothing worked. It was an unfathomable brain fart, worthy of a thousand bee stings.

But, I suppose, that's what I get for leaving New Hampshire. I'll never do that again.